"A fun and super   kers!"
—Sharon   n
Produc

"A thorough, dynamic, and inspiring guide for young film-makers written in the voice of a mentor who challenges but never underestimates her audience. It could be life-changing in the hands of a motivated teenager working on their own, and it's ideal as a text for high school media courses."
— Bruce Sheridan, professor and chair, Cinema Art and Science, Columbia College Chicago

"An engaging book for teens, and a wealth of informa-tion about movie making for all ages, now on our school must-read list for students and staff."
— Trevor Kolkea, principal, École Moody Middle School of the Arts

"A great tool! I wish I had it when I started my first film!"
— Eileen Hoeter, chair, Women in Film and Television International

"A helpful and detailed yet easy-to-read and understand guide for aspiring filmmakers—with a focus on teens. Using language younger creative minds can understand and engage with, Patz is ensuring the next generation of emerging screen-based artists is armed with the keys to success in the industry."
— Kim Hsu Guise, director of content, Local and Original Programming, TELUS

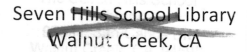

"You want to start making movies? You need this book! *Write! Shoot! Edit!* distills the complex process into doable bites and provides a lot of fun along the way."
  —Alex Raffe, vice-president production, Thunderbird Entertainment

"Three cheers for *Write! Shoot! Edit!* Better than a text book, this is a remarkable toolkit for any fledgling film-maker but teenagers in particular. Brilliantly engaging, encouraging and entertaining, it provides the how-to with professional know-how. *Chapeau!*"
  —Cheryl Wagner, creator of The Big Comfy Couch; executive director of The Charlottetown Film Festival

"Deborah Patz has written the book I wish I'd been handed as a young person; brilliant, funny and a very accurate introduction to all the mysteries of storytelling for the screen. I plan to revisit this one often!"
  —Karen Walton, Screenwriter, *Ginger Snaps*

WRITE! SHOOT! EDIT!

THE COMPLETE GUIDE TO FILMMAKING FOR TEENS

DEBORAH PATZ

MICHAEL WIESE PRODUCTIONS

Published by Michael Wiese Productions
12400 Ventura Blvd. #1111
Studio City, CA 91604
(818) 379-8799, (818) 986-3408 (FAX)
mw@mwp.com
www.mwp.com

Cover design by Johnny Ink. www.johnnyink.com
Interior design by William Morosi
Copyediting by David Wright
Printed by McNaughton & Gunn

Manufactured in the United States of America

Library of Congress Cataloging-in-Publication Data

Names: Patz, Deborah S., author.
Title: Write! shoot! edit! : the complete guide to filmmaking for teens / by
    Deborah Patz.
Description: Studio City, CA : Michael Wiese Productions, 2017. | Includes
    bibliographical references and index.
Identifiers: LCCN 2016052372 | ISBN 9781615932641 (alk. paper)
Subjects: LCSH: Motion pictures--Production and direction--Vocational
    guidance.
Classification: LCC PN1995.9.P7 P385 2017 | DDC 791.4302/32--dc23
LC record available at https://lccn.loc.gov/2016052372

Printed on Recycled Stock

Thanks to

Natalya, Katherine, Nicoletta, Michele, and Jonathan,

the very many fabulous folk who brought me to this place and time, especially Ken and Eva,

the amazing Michael and Ken
at Michael Wiese Productions,

my mom (for my wings in life),

and you . . .

the future of story!

Table of Contents

How to Use This Book

First up, *do not read this book in order*. Okay, you can if you really want to, and in any case, you do have to start with Chapter One. You see, this book has three distinct paths to create fiction movies and it's designed to be read and experienced from three different perspectives:

the **Writer**;

 the **Director** (and Director of Photography);

and

the **Editor**.

Each path is unique, and you'll discover that they weave and intersect with each other at different points along the way.

Ready to start your very first film project? Divvy up the roles among your friends and each of you start on your own path. There will be plenty of overlap and you're going to need a team anyway.

But maybe you want to tackle more than one role and become a hyphenate, like a Writer-Director: Follow each of the paths you choose. Along the way, you'll revisit a chapter or two; experience it the second time from your new perspective.

What if you shot some footage already and just need help to complete your film? Simple. Start with Chapter One and follow the Editor path.

Even teachers of early teens or young adults can use this book. Focus on one path, or divide the class up into teams and explore each of the three perspectives.

On which path are you going to start *your* cinematic journey?

Introduction

You're on set and framing the shot. Performers are in position, in character and waiting. Someone is holding a silver reflector at just the right angle to soften the shadow on their faces. The camera is ready and the microphone not visible in the shot. You nod to the person holding a mike off-screen. A smile is returned. Others around you are holding as still as possible. Everyone is waiting for your word. Your breath is tense in anticipation, your mouth a bit dry. The whole experience feels strange but also so very right. This is it! You're making your movie!

"Action!"

Filmmaking is not a solo act. Oh boy, you totally understand that on the first day of the shoot! You need a team to make it happen, so you'll be tapping into friends and family to make yours. It's also true that with the first films you make, you'll be "wearing plenty of hats" before the movie is completed. You won't have enough people to fill each role with a separate person. Naturally, that means you want to learn about as many of these perspectives as possible. Understand the power you have with each "hat" by looking at them separately, then bring that knowledge together—in your own brain or through a team of friends. This book provides you with enough information on the whole filmmaking process to start small, learn from your successes, then move on to bigger challenges. You can be part of the magic of movies . . . starting now!

Take me as an example: I shot my first film when I was 9: an ad lib 5-minute interview with the family dog, thanks to a couple of spoonfuls of peanut butter where he supplied the mouth movements and I supplied the voice for his responses. Moving up to a script, more performers and interior lighting, I then wrote and shot a scripted commercial for a can of beans. Why a can of beans? Well, because it was there in the cupboard! Next was a 5-minute mystery thriller where I experimented with implied footage and editing to create the illusion of a crime on screen. By the time I was in my later years at high school, I made a 20-minute action/murder mystery with the complexity of a large cast, plus many locations and stunts. That film helped me earn a spot in film school, after which

I've been working in the professional film industry (since the month I graduated) with companies like Disney, Lucasfilm, MCA/Universal, Alliance/Atlantis and many others. I've now had such diverse film-making experiences as having worked with the likes of Anthony Daniels (C-3PO of *Star Wars*), William Shatner (Captain Kirk of *Star Trek*), and all the Care Bears. I also spent time at a morgue (and it was a happy experience), sat on the Big Comfy Couch, and even sent a camera into space (yes, real space). Now I help my own kids and people like you, through workshops, to discover and experiment with the magic of movies to make their own stories. Your stories.

Professional feature films are typically between 90 and 120 minutes. Scale that down to a doable length for first films. Let's start with 12 minutes . . . or if this is your subsequent reading and you're ready for something more complex, 24 minutes. For either case, don't plan on public distribution (e.g., YouTube, Vimeo) for your finished film. Free yourself from copyright concerns. Experiment and enjoy the journey. You'll still have a premiere: a private one with friends and family and they'll be part of all those making-of inside jokes and woes, so it's going to be a blast.

Ready? Of course you are!

Chapter One

The Three-Headed Creative Process

Itching to make your movie? You've already imagined it: your words and images on the big screen with an audience watching, or on a portable screen in the palm of your hand. Am I right? Well, then, be ready to make it three times.

What?

Yup. A film story is created three times before making it to the theater or final destination. The good news is that it's also easier than it sounds because we break the process down into doable segments.

First written as a script, the story is imagined into being, from nothing. But even as a finished script, it's not a movie yet. It's words on a page. During the shoot, the story is brought to life with real world people, locations, images and sounds.

Performances are interpreted. Locations add details not imagined while writing. The script was the plan, but the film story has been re-imagined visually with added meaning and richness. It has evolved. Still, it's not a finished movie yet. It's a collection of separate shots. Finally, those unchangeable pieces are edited into order and re-ordered and re-imagined once again into the story's final, living form. The script may be the road map, but in the edit room the final, visual story is crafted and told.

Writing, shooting and editing: each stage requires creativity and ingenuity. Which one(s) interest you most?

Quite obviously, the Writer is the key player of the writing stage, although others, including Story Editor, can assist with the process.

For the shoot, it's a bit more complicated. Many people collaborate to visualize the story. Since the Director crafts and leads the creative vision and the Director of Photography (DOP) is the lead camera creative, combine these roles into the hyphenate: Director-DOP as the key player for the shoot. In this book, I'll use the term Director.

For the editing stage, there's a smaller team than during the shoot, including specialists for picture, sound, music and sound effects. We'll wrap this team into the term Editor as the key player for this final stage.

But before we leap in, take a quick look at the overall creative process. I'm talking about the process that's going on inside your brain. It has three stages, too. Let me explain.

For anyone who has done a little writing already, you're bound to be aware of the competing voices in your head. They're like shoulder angels: one says that what you're writing is fan-tabulous! while the other is ruthlessly criticizing your unfinished work. Their arguments make it hard to get the writing done, don't they?

Their arguments also reveal that there is more than one stage to the writing (and creative) process. It's true. There are actually three stages, or three "heads" as I like to say. I label them Wild Inventor Brain, Dr. Structure Editor, and Nitpicky Tweaker because the images these labels conjure help you work with them.

WILD INVENTOR BRAIN
Wild Inventor doesn't like to work "in the box" or play by the rules. It's the inventor with ideas that flow fast and plenty when inspired, so go out and inspire it. Go for a walk in the park. Lie in a bubble bath. Sit under the table instead of at the table. Be a little crazy. Wild Inventor understands crazy. If the ideas seem too off-the-wall, then you have Dr. Structure Editor voicing an opinion. Listen to Dr. S. too soon and sensitive Wild Inventor will shut down. Tell Dr. S. to sit aside for now; its time to speak

up will come. Let Wild Inventor complete the entire first draft, or plan out a series of radically angled shots, so that Dr. Structure has a complete something to look at and evaluate for the next stage of the creative process.

Figure 1. (A) My Wild Inventor Brain. (B) Draw your Wild Inventor Brain.

DR. STRUCTURE EDITOR

Dr. Structure is not so much an inventor as one who likes to play with what's there to make it better. Consequently, Dr. S. has earned a bad reputation for volunteering critical, internal feedback too early in the creative process. Oddly, during the structural edit phase, Dr. S. isn't nearly so ruthless when critiquing. It can see and develop the potential of your work using learned experiences and industry standards of story crafting. It loves to diagnose logic problems and cares more about overall story structure, like "is the character motivation working," than about fixing typos and formatting issues (which it leaves for Nitpicky Tweaker).

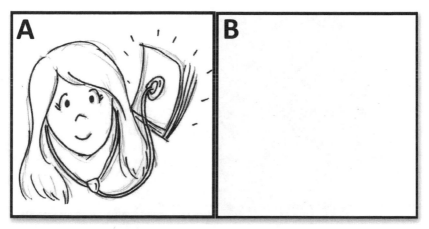

Figure 2. (A) My Dr. Structure Editor. (B) Draw your Dr. Structure Editor.

NITPICKY TWEAKER

For the Writer, Nitpicky is the copy editor, for Director and Editor, it's the polisher. No detail is too small for Nitpicky. It loves to dive into word choice, grammar and script format. It's the voice of exactness while framing a shot and the one who finds continuity errors between shots. It makes you trim that extra frame or two while editing so that shots flow together, or so that lip sync between sound and picture is corrected. Nitpicky cares about communicating the story as intended to the next in line . . . all the way to last in line: the audience. It's tempting to bring in

Nitpicky early, but let Dr. S. have a go before Nitpicky does a polish to finish the work.

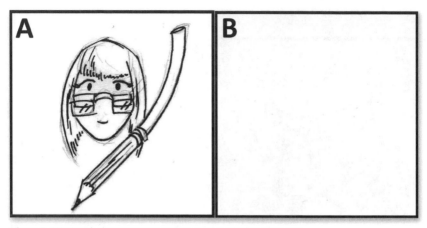

Figure 3. (A) My Nitpicky Tweaker. (B) Draw your Nitpicky Tweaker.

That's a lot going on in your head at the same time, isn't it?

Well, the trick is to keep these three heads working separately. Not entirely separately, but allow each one their time at center stage for their phase of the creative process. So, yes, it means if you're writing, you're going to have to write the script at least three times. If you're shooting or editing, you, too, will have to do your work three times: plan it, do it, tweak it.

By embracing this three-headed approach, you'll reduce the huge job ahead into doable chunks and tame the competing voices in your head along the way.

You and Your Path: The Writer, Director or Editor

Ready to choose your path? Let's look at your choices:

You as the Writer

You like to invent something from nothing. You see yourself collecting the Oscar for best original screenplay. When you walk the red carpet no one recognizes you, but at industry parties, insiders know you. You're more comfortable in a cozy sweater looking out the window at life with keyboard in front of you. On a tablet or scraps of paper, you capture notes that you plan to use in a story sometime. When you visit the set, you are doing just that: visiting. Watching performers bring your words to life gives you a charge. You are the Writer.

Wild Inventor will lead you through the first, discovery draft of the script, then Dr. Structure will take you through the development draft(s) and, finally, Nitpicky through the polish draft.

Yes, there is overlap in the stages. For example, although Nitpicky is the master of script format, you still need to know enough about that format to write the first, discovery draft. That's okay. Use proper format but be flexible. Let Wild Inventor lead you through that first draft to discover the story. Nitpicky can fix your formatting inconsistencies at time of polish. Need to tap into Dr. Structure's expertise of story and scene structure during the discovery draft? That's fine, too. Just don't allow that voice to judge your work until it's Dr. Structure's turn at center stage.

You as the Director

You count yourself a future peer of George Lucas, Steven Spielberg and Joss Whedon. You see yourself collecting the Oscar for best direction, and though you may be noticed on the red carpet, the fans aren't really there to see you (they want to see the stars you cast). At industry parties, filmies and producers flock around you to find out what picture you're doing next. You want to be interviewed for your role in making the movie and you're first to admit that it takes an incredible team to make it happen. You take inspiration from a good script and are energized by the challenge of turning it into real life sounds and images. You especially love to deconstruct the script's story with performers to find its deeper meaning. You see great locations, camera angles and visual meta-phors wherever you go. On set, the cast and crew look to you for leadership and you are the one to call "action" and "cut." You are the Director.

The shooting stage divides into prep, shoot, and wrap.

Wild Inventor leads you through designing a shot list—a plan to visualize the story in the script in preproduction ("prep"). Dr. Structure is the lead to shoot that shot list during principal photography (the "shoot"), addressing unforeseen circumstances that come up along the way, and Nitpicky pipes in regularly (at "wrap" of the shot, of the day, of the shoot) to ensure that the story is captured sufficiently for the Editor to finish the movie during the next stage.

Does it sound like these "heads" overlap each other more so than during writing? You're right. And each one needs its voice heard. Take choosing a location as an example: the scene in the script takes place backstage at a concert. Wild Inventor decides what needs to be seen on screen to make the audience believe we are truly backstage (without renting a concert hall which you can't afford). Dr. Structure finds and evaluates real life locations to make that vision come true, both scrounging and coming up with alternative, creative solutions. Nitpicky ensures there is sufficient access time to the location to capture the required shots, plus enough parking, power outlets, and lunch options nearby, if needed.

You as the Editor

If a movie is made three times, you want to be part of the last word in that path. You see yourself collecting the Oscar for best editing and don't mind sharing the accolade with a small team. You like to work with visual images but you don't have to be the one to shoot them. You like to play with the raw coverage, tweaking shot order, finding performance gems and basically fiddling with the work until it's just right. Because of that, the performances you hear in the edit room over and over again as you perfect a scene will linger in your memory for years to come and you'll repeat that dialogue *ad nauseam* to family and friends. You prefer to work alone and solicit feedback now and then. You can handle living in dark rooms even when it's sunny outside. Figuring out new technologies excites you. You know that picture editing is only half the process in postproduction (simply called "post" in the film industry) and you can't wait to experiment laying in tracks of sound and music. You already know which music to try because when you hear music, you feel it, and visuals spring instantly to mind. You are the Editor

Post is also made up of three stages: picture edit, sound edit, and the finish.

Most of the story crafting happens during the picture edit where Wild Inventor and Dr. Structure work rather closely together. From the existing footage, script, and continuity notes, Wild Inventor crafts a plan to build the final, filmed story. Dr. Structure comes in shortly thereafter to help with subsequent editing passes to better capture the story—its meaning and flow—with each pass. Nitpicky pops in during later edits to fine tune those choices.

Once the picture edit is "locked," sound layers are added with Dr. S. leading the way. Stealing dialogue from one take to lay it over the visual of another could be the way to use the best performances. Next, music and sound effects are layered in to add richness to the soundscape. Finally, Nitpicky leads the finishing stage to create output files that will play on technology of today and archive in a format that will play on the technology of tomorrow—whatever form that might be.

Now it's over to you. Which path are you going to take (today)?

 If you are following the path of Writer, go to
Chapter Two: Story Crafting and Character Creation (page 12).

 If you are following the path of Director, go to
Chapter Six: Preproduction: Designing the Shoot (page 59).

 If you are following the path of Editor, go to
Chapter Nine: The Last Word of Postproduction: Picture Post (page 113).

Chapter Two:
Story Crafting and Character Creation

Ideas. Whether you're swimming with them or need some, the first stop is to look at your life. That's where you'll find the best stories. Really. I'm not saying that filming what you had for breakfast will make good cinema, but, well . . . let me explain.

There are two layers to story. The action plot where a character is on screen doing stuff: defeating a villain, solving a mystery, or something else visual. Layered on and woven into that action is an interesting character. It's a human, somewhat like ourselves, and the reason we care to watch the action.

A bumbling cop (not just any cop) solves the mystery. The last pick for the sports team wins the game. An underdog hero defeats a bad guy. We follow interesting, human characters overcoming challenges because we are interesting, human characters who overcome challenges in our lives, too.

That's why movies can be so inspiring. Many of the best ones are based on life experiences we can relate to. It's those human experiences, those emotions, that echo within us and connect us to the characters and their stories on screen.

Connect Wild Inventor Brain to those experiences and let's go!

Gathering Ideas

You probably already have plenty of ideas. Creative people often do. Bet they're not all related to the movie you currently want to write, so keep an idea file (either on paper or electronically) for future projects. In case you do need a little inspiration or want to shake up the way you usually inspire yourself, here are a couple of techniques and locations to help you dream up story fragments, interesting situations and fascinating characters.

Freewrite: Freewriting is the number one technique to trigger Wild Inventor Brain. Sure, you can use a computer, but you'll find ideas flow better with pen or pencil and paper. It's harder to backspace on paper so Dr. S. is less likely to voice criticism and you can keep moving forward. Now, write. Forget about spelling, grammar, punctuation and English teachers. Just write. Don't stop. Don't judge. Time yourself for, say, 10 or 15 minutes and go. You'll be amazed what great material makes it onto the page. Use a starting line or word if you want to focus the freewrite, or just let Wild Inventor tell you what it wants to tell you.

Play "What if" or "I Remember": When freewriting stalls, this technique proves its worth. Write "what if" or "I remember" and let Wild Inventor complete the sentence. "What if" is also useful to take something existing and turn it into something new. What if . . . I had a time machine and used it to visit my 7-year-old self? What if . . . Middle C could really be stolen from the music scale? We know what Middle C sounds like. What would it look like? Ooo, the possibilities!

The News: Check out news headlines or stories for inspiration. Add a little "what if" or freewrite to see what new spin you can put on the story.

Dreams and 'Tween Time: Best to keep a pencil and paper beside the bed. As soon as you wake, jot down what you remember. It's amazing how quickly dream memories fade as we rouse. Beyond dreams, ideas naturally flow during that 'tween time as you're falling asleep. Your mind is at rest . . . well, until that fabulous idea floats in and then you end up arguing with yourself: will you remember the idea the next morning or not? Use the paper beside the bed and "write the idea away." Release your mind from having to remember it all night long and you'll drift off to sleep in no time.

Group Brainstorming: Use this technique to expand on idea fragments you already have. Gather your friends to bat around ideas. See what cool plot, situation, or characters come up.

Story Prompts via Cards, Cubes, Books or Websites: Gosh, you can find story prompts pretty much everywhere. They can be a deck of cards with images or words on them that you can shuffle and reveal in any order, or dice with graphics on each side instead of numbers, or books and websites with topics to write about or the first line of a story you can finish. What's important is that they all invoke you to play as a way to discover story. Use them in a freewrite session as a trigger to mine experiences from your life. Maybe the prompts you have are fantasy-based, not about real life. So what! Look at your life in metaphor. Imagine being royalty or a warrior or a court jester for those experiences of yours. Use prompts by yourself or campfire-style with friends to build a story from person to person.

Movies You've Seen: Don't copy what you've seen, but go ahead and be inspired. What detail or situation interested you? How would you do it differently? Perhaps you want to try a parody where Double-0-7 becomes a teen spy called Triple-0-7. Want to try your hand at an unexplored sequel or prequel? Go ahead! Explore the life of a minor character, like Henchman #2. What's his story?

Change Your Scene or Perspective: Are you physically restless? Go for a walk somewhere. Take a notepad with you. Perhaps you gravitate toward nature; a forest or a beach. When you're there, really look around and listen. Imagine a scene unfolding before you. Or if you choose to stay indoors, change your perspective. As mentioned before, try sitting under the table instead of at it. Pets are under there all the time. How do they see life? Let your mind wander . . . anywhere!

Trigger the Senses: The sense of smell is especially closely linked to memory, so smell stuff! Close your eyes, sniff and let Wild Inventor paint you a scene. To what time or location are you transported? Try again with touch: a downy feather, a crusty leaf, a chewed pencil. Try again with music (preferably instrumental). With eyes closed, what scene do you see? What do you remember?

Bet your ideas are flowing now!

When you stall in the creative process, come back here. Try these techniques again. They'll help you get unstuck. As for the ideas you do have, I bet you have some good ones! You may not have all the parts of a story yet, but that's okay. It's time to grow them into a story.

Growing Ideas into Stories

The unwritten story idea is beautiful. Pristine. You have a fabulous character or two, a cool situation. You can even imagine a couple of great lines. Untarnished by reality, the idea sparkles like a jewel in your mind. Yet jewels start as raw gems that are analyzed and cut to release the sparkle within. Drill into the details of your story idea and you'll find only raw fragments at the moment, not a complete story. That's natural. Prepare to develop and grow the idea into a story. Prepare to find the sparkle within.

Start with a one-liner. It's similar to a tagline and log line used by professional productions. You've already seen taglines on movie posters; their purpose is to entice the audience in a minimum number of words. Log lines are also brief but are used by producers to sell the movie to investors before it's made (so log lines contain more story description than do taglines). The one-liner is a bit like a log line in that its purpose is to summarize really briefly what your story is, but designed to keep you on track while writing. You'll find yourself repeating the one-liner time and again during production as you bring people on board and need to tell them about the story . . . briefly. Here's what to include:

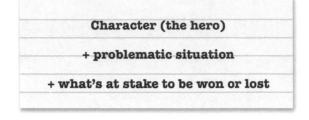

Character (the hero)

+ problematic situation

+ what's at stake to be won or lost

For example:

> Two pop star spies
>
> must track down the villain who stole Middle C
>
> before their benefit concert is canceled.

Notice a few things in the one-liner. The hero must actively do something. The hero cannot continue life without fixing the problem or solving the mystery. Both hero and villain are connected, and often there is a time limit to add to the peril. Distill some movies you've watched down to one-liners for practice, then tackle your own and post it over your writing desk as a reminder to keep you focused.

Now for a few more elements to push beyond the one-liner. Keep Wild Inventor's sense of play and direct your creative exploration to muse and build on any of the following ingredients that you find missing from your story idea:

(1) The Main Character (the "Hero"): The hero is the focus of the story and is part of the one-liner. The term "hero" sounds larger than life. Exactly right! Human like us but a bit more extreme. When you think about it, you are the hero of your own life. Now take a moment to describe what you know about your story's hero so far. We'll push this character to be even more interesting in the next sections.

I'll be using a female character as the Hero in the examples that follow, but as you know, heroes can be of any gender (or of any species, for that matter). When you read a specific pronoun, like "he" or "she," recognize the choice was made for consistency to help with understanding, and feel free to make your heroes, villains, henchmen and best friends whichever gender you wish.

(2) The Hero's Want and Desire (Character Motivation): What the hero wants is also part of the one-liner. We have to be able to see it: a physical object (real like a jewel, or invented like Middle C); or a person or animal (a dog); or to solve a mystery (the criminal is physically caught). Why the hero wants it is also important. The "why" is a secret desire and it comes from the hero's back story. What happened in the hero's past that led to something missing? Know the desire, and you know what motivates her and what choices she'll make in any scene. The desire is less tangible than the want, less visual: a wish to meet the hero's idol at the benefit concert; or to feel like her family is complete (by having a dog); or to earn respect of her cop colleagues (by finally solving a case).

(3) Why Can't the Hero Have the Desire? (Conflict): Here's where the hero comes into conflict with the villain. The villain actively prevents the hero from obtaining her desire—by stealing Middle C, by kidnapping the parents, by being too crafty a criminal to be caught.

(4) What Does the Hero Have to Do? (Actions, Events, Friends, Mentors): This question fuels much of the action and events in the story. The hero makes friends and enemies and discovers competitors. Mentors guide the way. The villain doesn't just show up at the end; he is there at the beginning and pursuing a want of his own that happens to conflict with the hero's. Jot down ideas of events that could happen and other characters the hero could meet.

(5) Final Face-Off Alone (Climax): The hero faces the villain alone. This face-off is the climactic scene we've been waiting for since the start of the movie. We want to see how far the hero has come to face such an adversary and triumph. We are here to see the hero out-fight, out-wit and/or out-logic the villain.

(6) How the Story Ends (Resolution): The ending relates back to the hero's desire. Although chasing a physical want, the hero earns her less tangible desire by the end of the story. The desire fulfilled may not be in the form of the original desire, but it's better and it's awesome. The pop stars' benefit concert is a success, plus their idol becomes personal friends with them. The hero realizes her family is complete with or without a dog, plus together they start a dog-sitting business. The cop solves the case, is awarded a medal, plus wins her boyfriend's heart.

Since it's clear that characters make the action happen, let's zoom in on them for a bit.

Characters Beyond Stereotypes

Think about movies you've seen. It's the characters you remember, right? Great lines they deliver, cool things they do. That's what you want for your story: memorable characters—ones that are fun to perform and entertaining to watch. Move from black and white to dark and light gray. Huh? Let me explain.

It's tempting to grab a couple of stereotypes and go. You know how "they" will act in any given situation: the science nerd, the dumb jock. Bit of a boring choice, no? We, as people, are more than these kinds of labels. We have desires, weaknesses and quirks that don't necessarily align with a given stereotype, so why limit our characters?

Add flaws to the good guys. We'll recognize those weaknesses in ourselves and feel connected to them. Don't stop there. Give sympathetic qualities to the bad guys, so we feel a little bit for them, too.

Adding this type of complexity is food for writing. The villain can exploit the hero's weakness to win the upper hand, while also going to great lengths to hide his own flaw. Their skills, flaws, desires and quirks help characters react in a more surprising and enter-taining manner. Move beyond stereotypical norms.

To do so, here's the minimum you need for each main character:

Name: Since you're not planning on publicly distributing your movie, you can name your characters anyway you like. If you're considering public distribution, use first names only. Believe it or not, people own their own names and filmmakers cannot use them without permission. The more unique the name, the easier it is to identify its owner. Instead, by using generic first names, like "John" or "Sally," it's impossible to identify an owner, so you don't need permission.

Want: The action story follows the hero going after a want, a physical thing. It could be a dog, a missing brother, a crown, lots of money, a trophy, etc. Give other main characters wants too, even if they are secret wants, never revealed. A very short film won't have the screen time to explore them all, but knowing them will help you answer story questions as you write, like "how would so-and-so react here?"

Desire: Although it sounds like a want, a desire is different and deeper. It's the reason for the (physical) want. The character wants a dog because she thinks the dog will make her family complete. Her desire, then, is for a complete family. The hero has a want at the beginning of the movie and wins the desire by the end of the movie. Other main characters can have desires too, even if they are never revealed.

If the characters you dream up seem too unreal compared with your everyday life (a pop star, astronaut, millionaire, superhero), then simply add wants and desires from your own life. Do you yearn for a pet you're not allowed to have? Give that yearning to the pop star character who can't have one due to the pop star lifestyle. Now you both have a connection. You've humanized her and can more easily write her. The audience, too, will connect with that yearning. That's what it means to "write what you know."

Skills, Flaws and Quirks: Here's another place to connect your life to your characters and make writing them easier. Give your lead and support characters skills, flaws and quirks that you yourself know. For skills, any kind is useful. Really. Flaws are your characters' temptations that lead them into trouble in the story. Quirks are oddities and superstitions. Here's a list to start you off. Customize it for you to use in this story or the next. (See Figure 4.)

Write! Shoot! Edit! CHARACTER BUILDING BEYOND STEREOTYPES		
Skills	Flaws	Quirks
Swim fast	Interrupts people	Never uses red paperclips
Sail blindfolded	Weakness for chocolate	Won't sleep under a full moon
Play chess	Weakness for 70% off sales	Uses two alarm clocks to wake
Hold breath for 3 minutes	Must pet dogs at the park	Must put right shoe on first
Ride a horse backwards	Games excessively	Books at home are alphabetized
Identify types of rocks	Shy	Carries spare batteries

Figure 4. Make your own reference chart of skills, flaws and quirks to push characters beyond stereotypes.

If you're not into making lists, then note skills, flaws and quirks on separate cards, shuffling them to create your characters by random order. Keep Wild Inventor playing and discovering awesome characters.

I haven't talked much about physical character description (age, gender, height and such). Yes, you need a short description of each character, but you'll be casting from your circle of friends and family, so an extensive description is not necessary. You're making a movie, not writing a book. The character qualities (from wants to quirks) will be the useful bits to help your cast get into character during the shoot.

The Roles Characters Play

So, how many of these awesome characters are you going to need? It depends on your story and how many people you have access to for filming. The real question is how many roles do the characters play to tell the story?

The Hero: Obviously you need one of these. The hero is the lead character or protagonist. We follow the hero through her story from wanting something at the beginning to being rewarded at the end. The hero needs a want, desire, skill, flaw and quirk.

The Villain: A necessary evil (pun intended). Also known as the antagonist, the villain actively tries to prevent the hero from getting what she wants, so by contrast, the villain and hero are closely linked. The stronger the villain is (physically or intellectually), the more amazing the hero will be when the villain is defeated. Give the villain a want that contrasts with the hero's, and because of the hero-villain link, add a skill, flaw and quirk too.

The Mentor: This character is someone who teaches the hero how to face the villain, but can't be there to help when the inevitable hero-villain confrontation happens (because the mentor is either dead or otherwise absent). Although wizened old men with long beards come to mind, a mentor can be anyone of any age. Obviously, the mentor has a skill. Give her a want, flaw and quirk too.

The Best Friend: The hero's sidekick typically appears to be less courageous than the hero, but is solidly at the hero's side through adversity. He may try to tempt the hero into not facing the villain in order to play it safe. Although it's the flaw that rules the best friend's decisions, add a want, skill and quirk, too.

Lead Henchman: The villain often has a sidekick who helps take care of nefarious duties. Somewhat like the best friend is to the hero, the henchman is typically subservient to the villain, not on equal social standing. This character is useful to provide dialogue potential so the villain can voice his plans aloud for the audience to hear. Give the henchman a want, skill, flaw and quirk.

There are many other possible roles. Search and study archetypes and mythologies if you want to dive in for more. Friends and allies are helpers that the hero meets along the way, but may only have a brief appearance. Enemies or competitors are characters that hinder the hero's path. The sufferer or victim is someone who always seems to have bad luck. The trickster will change sides to suit her needs. The love interest . . . well, that one's obvious.

Roles are also very flexible so that several characters can take one on. Alternatively, one character can play several roles, morphing from one into another as the story progresses. The comic relief, for example, often doubles up with the best friend or lead henchman. What if an ally betrays the hero and becomes one of the villain's henchmen? What if the villain is disguised as the mentor at the beginning? Mix and match to your heart's delight. Experiment!

Action-Reaction Zigzag Outlining

Before we invite Dr. Structure Editor to help with a full-on look at story structure, linger a bit longer with Wild Inventor Brain. Zigzag outlining is more idea discovery than story planning.

Plot, you see, is not a straight line. The hero would like it to be a straight line: hero wants a dog, hero gets a dog. Now *that* would make a very boring movie. Don't be so kind to your hero. Make her life really difficult along the way. Take your hero on a roller coaster of ups and downs.

We know from physics that for every action there is an equal and opposite reaction. Add physics to your action plot. Cause and effect make story. The first action causes a reaction. The reaction causes a new action. The new action causes another reaction, and so on. Zigzag back and forth between highs and lows, or ups and downs, and you have a roller coaster of causal events.

Let's add zigzag to the boring hero-wants-a-dog story:

Hero yearns for a dog (it's sad; down). Parents gift a pet to the hero (yay! up). But the pet is a cat (darn; down).

Down-up-down-up. See how the events link? Make the causal links as tight as possible, by starting each new action or reaction with "Because of . . . . " (See Figure 5.)

On it goes. Keep zigzagging events, folding in new characters and complicating the plot on its way to the final outcome: a reward better than what was originally desired. In this case, perhaps the hero realizes she's a cat person after all, or the hero earns both a cat and a dog.

What you're actually doing is adding obstacles and conflict to the plot. Just don't go easy on your hero. Push her to the limit! In life, how we handle ourselves in crisis and conflict shows our true character. Do the

Write! Shoot! Edit! ZIGZAG OUTLINING		
Causal Event	**Emotional Feeling**	**Why That Feeling?**
Because of the cat, the hero plans to trade pets with a friend	Up!	Hope for hero's desire
Because of the plan, the hero ends up in a dangerous situation	Down...	Danger!
Because of the danger, the cat rescues the hero	Up!	Surprising friendship
Because of the rescue, the cat ends up in danger instead	Down...	Hero feels guilty; cat in danger
Because the cat's in danger, the hero meets a new friend	Up!	Hope for friendship
Because of meeting the new friend, a crime ring is exposed	Down...	More danger!
Because the crime ring is exposed, (etc.)	Up!	
	Down...	

Figure 5. An example of zigzag outlining to discover the story.

same for your hero. Make her earn the reward at the end of the movie. We want to know that, given the similar stresses, we could act as well as the hero and so, too, earn an equivalent reward.

Each event is bound to be more fleshed out in your mind than such brief descriptions as I've shown here. That's outlining. Jot down quick summaries and move on. Keep the story moving forward, uh, I mean *zigzagging* forward.

It's now time for Dr. Structure Editor to take center stage. Wild Inventor Brain is still around and contributing, but Dr. S. is in a better position to step back, evaluate what you have, and bring out its potential to make it even better. Feeling a bit overwhelmed yet? Remember that you don't have to tackle everything in each movie you make. Pick and choose what you want to work on. Keep it achievable and move forward.

Since you are following the path of Writer, on to the next chapter!

Chapter Three:

Screenwriting to the Power of Three

Surrounded by scribbles on scraps of paper or fragmented notes on a computer? You've been exploring story without form until now. Put on the hat of Dr. Structure Editor and let's tame those fragments into traditional movie story structure.

First up, place your scraps of notes aside, but nearby. Grab a stack of index cards (or scraps of paper about that size). Clear yourself a space you can use to create a timeline. It could be a bulletin board, a space on the floor you can use for a few days, or a dining table if your family prefers to eat in the kitchen anyway.

You can do this work in a single document on the computer if you want, but there is something inspiring about tangibly moving index cards around and seeing the entire story laid out before you. Try cards at least once for the structuring process.

Summarize one scene per card and lay each down in their appropriate place in the timeline.

The 3-Act Structure in Four Parts

Three is a magic number. Don't movies know it! They all share a very satisfying three-act structure:

- **Act One**—the introduction and setup
- **Act Two**—the roller coaster ride of events
- **Act Three**—the final confrontation and wrap up (of loose ends)

Granted, features are typically 90 to 120 minutes long. How is that going to help you? Well, one page of a script equals about one minute of screen time. Distill a 120-minute feature into a 12-minute short and there's no problem! You can write a 12-page script.

Ready? Divide your timeline space into four sections. That's right, I said four, not three. Act Two is twice as long as acts One and Three, and there are differences between its two halves.

Act One—30 pages for a feature, 3 pages for you:

Act One opens with a twist, an event that kick-starts the story. The hero is going about her normal life when a dilemma is discovered, or a crime committed.

During Act One, use the scenes to introduce major characters and their motivations. What makes them tick? What's missing in their lives? Especially focus on the hero's and villain's lives. You don't want major characters arriving for the first time in Act Three or your story will feel contrived and the audience will feel cheated. Introduce all the major ones now. If they can't be on screen in Act One, at least talk about them. Introduce them by reputation.

This idea of "introduce now" applies to coincidence too. Any coincidental event that happens in your story should happen only in Act One or, again, the story will feel contrived.

Act One also ends with a twist or big reveal. The hero can no longer live a normal life. Perhaps the first clue is discovered, or the hero transported into an alternate world. Make it big. Think cliffhanger at the end of a chapter in a good book.

First half of Act Two—30 pages for a feature, 3 pages for you:

Both halves of Act Two are the bumpy roller coaster ride of the story. If the hero is an odd duck in the environment, then it's here in Act Two where we see that contrast and laugh, cry, sigh, cheer, and so on. Use your zigzag outlining to its fullest.

It's possible to meet a new character or two early in this act, especially if the character has moved from one world into another, but typically we're talking about supporting characters, not major ones.

The first half of Act Two ends in the midpoint. It's another plot twist and often a low point for the hero. Reveal something important or complicate the hero's life in some dramatic way. Perhaps the real identity of the villain is exposed, or the extent of the villain's plans are uncovered. It's also possible for the hero to meet the villain in a small confrontation and lose. What's happened up until now is that the hero has been reacting to events that happen to her. Chances are the hero has been one step behind the villain for the first half of Act One. The midpoint event makes it clear that the hero can no longer react, but instead has to take charge and act from now on (whether she wants to or not) to head toward that inevitable, final confrontation with the villain.

Second half of Act Two—30 pages for a feature, 3 pages for you:
The bumpy roller coaster of a ride continues for the second half of Act Two. For this half, the hero is more in charge of her destiny, making decisions, learning, doing.

At the end of Act Two there is another twist, but this one is a dark one. It's the lowest point in the hero's life. There is loss, betrayal and/or abandonment. Typically, the mentor character is removed (through absence or death or other inevitable excuse). The hero has been amassing strength and friends in Act Two, but so too has the villain. For the upcoming climax, we want the hero and villain to face off alone. We want to see the hero's inner strength triumph, not have friends fly in and save her. That's why the hero has to lose all new-found support in this act. Bring the hero to the verge of quitting. We know in our hearts that quitting will not be the option, because the hero is, well, heroic.

Act Three—30 pages for a feature, 3 pages for you:

Stripped of helpers, the hero knowingly faces the villain anyway in Act Three. This is the confrontation scene that we've been waiting for all movie! At the start, the hero and villain were likely not equal to each other. The hero needed to learn and grow, and now in Act Three, they are equals (whether or not the hero believes it yet). What has the hero learned that can be used against the villain? The pop stars have learned to outwit the clever Middle C villain. The bumbling cop has learned how to catch the criminal red-handed this time.

Any surprises that happen at the climax must be hinted at earlier in the story so the audience can look back and see the seeds of that surprise (and so feel smart that they saw them).

After the climax comes a feel-good moment of resolution. The hero may or may not win her want by the end of the story, but will definitely win something better: the hero's secret desire.

The presumption here is that the ending will be uplifting, happy. If you want a downer ending instead, invert the highs and lows. Take the lowest point at end of Act Two and make it the most optimistic moment in the hero's life. When we see she's clearly on the path to winning all she wants and desires, flip the circumstances at the climax. The upbeat moment at end of Act Two was merely an illusion. Both hero and audience will feel the terrible slide from near win to total loss.

How is your timeline doing? Well populated with cards? Keep flexible. The page numbers I mention are guidelines (not rules) to help keep the story moving forward. For a bit of fun research, watch a feature film with a clock and watch the three-act structure play out . . . in four parts.

The Magic of Threes

The magic of threes needs further mention. With it, you can turn a coincidence in Act Three into a satisfying surprise. Just as the entire story plays out in three acts, use a recurring element three times over the course of the story. The recurrence lays sufficient groundwork for a well-crafted surprise reveal late in the story.

Scene in Act One: The hero annoys the best friend because she stops to pet dogs all the time.

Scene in Act Two: The villain uses a dog in the park to lure the hero into a trap.

Scene in Act Three: The villain's dog betrays the villain for the hero at a pivotal climatic moment.

Set up the recurring element (introduce it). Develop the recurring element (use it in a new way). Use the recurring element (the "surprising" reveal).

A scene is also made up of three parts: (1) enter the scene [the introduction], (2) the interaction [the ride], and (3) leave the scene [the wrap-up]. I'll cover more on using and manipulating scene structure in Chapter Five.

The Mirror Moment

We love it when stories come full circle. Watch a good movie and you know when you've arrived at the final scene. Perhaps you're sad that it's over, but you know the end when you see it. The reason for this feeling is the mirror moment.

The end of the story mirrors the start. Effectively it's a location, an action or a line of dialogue that's exactly the same at both beginning and end. Okay, not exactly the same. The hero has changed. The hero's world may be different. But, like a mirror, it's a reflection. The same but different. It could be as specific as a line with modified phrasing, such as: "I will never have a dog" becomes "I will never not have a dog." Or it could be the exact same line with new meaning, like "I need you" (to help with homework) becomes "I need you" (to be part of my life). Alternatively, the mirror moment can encompass an entire scene. The pop stars plan to invite their own idol and inspiration to their concert in Scene One, and then they meet their idol backstage at the end when she not only attends, but also performs with them.

Because of the mirror moment, you may end up modifying your first scene after writing the last scene. How can you make your story come full circle, too?

Are movie scenes playing out in your head now? They probably are. It's time to introduce you to script format.

 Since you're following the path of Writer, continue on!

Chapter Four:

Prepping the Script for the Shoot

For a movie, there is a very particular script format.

As Writer, it's time to transfer scenes from head to paper. For movies, script format is very particular because the story needs to be divisible into shootable segments—scenes— that can be re-ordered to work with the shooting schedule.

As Director, you need to understand the flow and meaning of the entire story, too. You also need to decide on the pieces necessary for each scene (when you shoot them out of order) so the meaning and flow are revealed when order is restored in the edit room. Believe it or not, script format helps.

Proper script format is in the realm of Nitpicky Tweaker—which is why I didn't talk about format too soon. Wild Inventor starts the story creation process, but is not big on established form.

The Script Format Road Map

Yes, you can buy or download scriptwriting software that takes care of format for you, but it's not necessary. Such software is terrific if you write scripts frequently, but you are doing more than just writing a script. There's a learning curve for that software to modify a script for, and during, a shoot. Instead, with the right set of tabs, you can start and end in a word processor (like Word or Pages) with no learning curve and tons of flexibility. Use these tab settings:

0 (left margin) = Scene headings and action description

1 inch = Dialogue

2 inches = Parentheticals (rarely used descriptions of how to say dialogue)

2.5 inches = Name of character saying the dialogue

5 inches = Transitions (like "DISSOLVE TO")

In Figures 6 and 7, see how the format looks in use.

```
                Write! Shoot! Edit! (title, centered)
                     by Writer Name
                        [Date]

FADE IN:

1 - EXT - LOCATION - DAY

 A CHARACTER is doing some action. Description of action is minimal
and in the present tense. OTHER CHARACTER does action too.
Capitalize their names when they first appear.

                        CHARACTER NAME
                Though my Character Name looks centered,
                it's really 3 tabs from the left margin,
                and dialogue starts at 1 tab in.

                        OTHER CHARACTER NAME
                What about at 2 tabs?

                        CHARACTER NAME
                     (whispers)
                The rare parenthetical when you have to
                describe to the performer how to say the line.

Other Character nods.

                        CHARACTER NAME (CONT)
                Numbering scenes is not necessary for the
                first draft. Add them only on the final draft.

                        OTHER CHARACTER NAME
                Right-o. And we must use Courier 12 font.

                        CHARACTER NAME
                Exactly. That's so that one script page
                equals about one minute of screen time.

2 - INT - LOCATION - NIGHT

The room is dim. The clock reads 9:15. Character and Other Character
drink tea.
```

Figure 6. An example of script format, page one.

Write! Shoot! Edit! - [Date] - 2

OTHER CHARACTER NAME
What does "INT" and "EXT" mean?

CHARACTER NAME
Interior and exterior. Useful so the shooting crew can group similar scenes together and not spend the shoot day going inside and outside and inside again at locations.

DISSOLVE TO:

3 - INT - LOCATION - NIGHT (LATER)

The clock now reads 11:25. Twenty empty tea cups litter the coffee table.

OTHER CHARACTER NAME
...and that about covers my questions.

CHARACTER NAME
"For now" you mean, don't you?

Other character smiles.

FADE OUT.

Figure 7. An example of script format, page two.

From Discovery to Polishing to Revisions

Don't be afraid to write the script a few times. The first draft of the script is the discovery draft. Tapping mostly into Wild Inventor, it's the draft where you just need to capture the story on paper and not worry too much about script format being perfect. You can even handwrite in approximate script format at this stage. Not being tied to a computer screen, where it is increasingly difficult to edit as you write, keeps Wild Inventor in charge.

Next come the development drafts. Evaluate what you have and incorporate input from yourself and others who have read your work. Not all your changes will be story-related. Some changes will come out of life's realities. The Director brings this valuable perspective. Something written may be physically impossible to shoot. Your friend who was going to play the villain has become unavailable, so you have to rewrite the villain to be played by one of your parents, who is available.

Finally, when you feel production-ready, trigger Nitpicky to validate your scene breaks, add scene numbers and take care of any fine tuning of details and dialogue in a final polish.

If you have to revise the script after shooting has begun, parts of the script will be shot already (unchangeable). Use an asterisk in the right margin to mark each line affected by the rewrite. Also include the date of the revision in the header of the revised page(s). (See Figure 8.)

Write! Shoot! Edit! - Revised [Date] - [Page Number]

3 - INT - LOCATION - NIGHT (LATER)

The clock now reads 1:40. Forty empty tea cups and an open,   *
empty tin of hot chocolate litter the coffee table.   *

> OTHER CHARACTER NAME
> ...and that about covers my questions.

Figure 8. For revisions, mark revised lines in the right margin with asterisks.

When Does a Scene Change?

Give the Writer a break! Busy writing the story, the Writer may not always be accurate with proper scene breaks. The Director can assist to polish the shooting script with correct scene breaks . . . since the Director has to handle and film each scene separately anyway.

A new scene starts when there is a change in location or a change in time. Sounds easy until you find yourself asking questions about gray areas, like: "Is moving from the living room to dining room a new scene or not? They're both interior house!" The final answer lies with the Director who is busy visualizing the story from the script road map. Will you shoot the living room and dining room in the same house or will you use a living room in one person's house and a dining room in another person's house? Make the decision and slot in the new scene heading (or not) where it should go.

If you're not sure when to make an elapsed-time scene break, ask yourself: "Can I keep the camera rolling and the action will be continuous?" If yes, it's one scene. In the example above, the numerous empty cups must be placed on the coffee table during an interval, so a new scene heading is warranted. Clothing changes are another typical signifier for an elapsed-time scene break.

Reading the Script as a Director, Not a Writer

As you can see, the Director starts to play a role in the last stages of script creation. The new perspective is especially visual, because the words-on-a-page of the script is not the final destination for the story.

See a lot of white space on a script page? Use it to make notes. Sketch line drawings of shots that you see in your mind's eye. Think comic book. Don't worry if you draw stick figures. The memory prompts are by you and for you. Pencil in camera directions too, if you like.

See each scene of the script as a separate part. What elements do you need to shoot each one? If the character picks up a bouquet of flowers, you need a bouquet of flowers in that scene. Write it down. Use colored pencils or highlighters or draft a list of requirements in a separate document. These notes and lists are known as the script breakdowns. You'll refer to them in prep to gather the necessary elements. For each scene identify:

1. **Scene number**

2. **Location** (remember that a living room, dining room and kitchen don't have to be in the same house)

3. **Characters** (include implied ones who have to be on camera but may not have dialogue and so are not specifically mentioned in the scene)

4. **Props** (objects that the characters interact with, touch or pick up)

5. **Special notes** (notes about pretty much anything you don't normally have at home, like unique clothing, animals, special lighting needs, script-specified weather, and so on)

You may not know how to shoot everything yet. That's fine. You've created a "to-visualize" list. The Director and team will invoke Wild Inventor to puzzle out how to shoot each item on the list or determine if a script revision is necessary to remove an impossible item or two.

If you are following the path of Writer, go to
Chapter Five: Your Visual Storytelling Toolbox (page 46).

If you are following the path of Director, go to
Chapter Seven: Preproduction: Juggling the Logistics (page 85).

Chapter Five:

Your Visual Storytelling Toolbox

It's no secret (by now) that the script is not the final destination for the story. Filmmaking is visual storytelling with the script as first step in planning that visual story. Creative decisions made during the shoot and editing play just as big a part as crafting the original story. Each stage is creative and magic.

This chapter introduces you to a whole slew of concepts to improve your visual storytelling no matter which perspective you choose. Consider it a visual storytelling toolbox to help strengthen the bond between screen and audience. Pick and choose what you want to experiment with and go for it! No need to tackle everything in a first attempt. There are many movies inside you!

Discover this chapter from your current perspective—as Writer, Director or Editor—then come back again to experience it through different eyes.

Visualizing a Scene in Three Parts

A scene is made up of three parts. Yes, another "three." In this case:

1. **Entrance**

2. **Interaction, and**

3. **Exit**

Makes you think of the stage, doesn't it? Performers walk onto the stage for each scene, act out the scene and then leave the stage. To cheat the necessary logistics of entering and exiting for every scene, performers can enter or exit with the curtain drawn or lights off. What's interesting here is that they're trying to remove the entrance and exit where possible. That's good advice. Home in as soon as possible on the meat of the scene: the interaction.

You'd be bored silly if you had to watch every scene in a movie play out all three parts all the time. A character says, "Let's go to lunch." and as the audience, you want to be at that lunch in the next shot. You don't want to watch the group of people stand up, put on coats and sweaters, leave the room, travel, arrive at the restaurant, hang up coats and sweaters, find a table, figure out who sits where, and on and on. Ugh! "Let's go to lunch." Cut to: Everyone already seated in the restaurant. Fabulous food is being placed before them. "Now that's what I call lunch." We move from interaction in one scene to interaction in another.

Now, if the entrance or exit has a story reason to be there, by all means keep it. They plan to go to lunch, but when they open the door to leave, a mysterious person is there. It's a person they would not have met unless they were exiting the room. You need this moment. It's a moment of story discovery. If the new mysterious person is already seated with them at the restaurant, the audience will "come out of the story" to wonder how and why the new person is there. In their loss of connection to the story they won't listen as closely to the dialogue and so miss more of the story. Show moments of discovery on screen.

Are there any scenes in your story that can have entrances and/or exits trimmed? Perhaps you want to experiment with cutting from an entrance in one scene to an exit in another.

So, how do you know what part(s) to keep? Look for the moments of change.

Scenes: There's Meaning in the Change

In each scene, at least one of the characters has to undergo some kind of change. I'm not talking about the big change that happens to the hero over the course of the movie. (You need that, too.) A change-within-a-scene is smaller: learn new information, be betrayed, be faced with a dilemma. Something like that. These moments of change are small and incremental. Together they add up to that big change at the end, giving each scene story meaning—a reason to be in the movie. If there is no change in a scene, the story will feel static, not moving. The audience will become bored. Keep the story moving.

The change, by the nature of the medium, is visual. We see it play out in the actions and reactions of the performers, especially in their eyes.

The pop star spies check in with their spy manager and learn about the thief's evil plot. They learn something in the scene: a surveillance photo (visual, physical evidence) that explains why their world recently changed (Middle C was stolen). By the end of the scene, they have changed from being curious to being determined to chase down and stop the thief. The story moves forward.

Look at each scene in your movie. Identify the change in each one. If nothing changes, chances are you don't need that scene in the movie. Cut it now and save yourself from filming it only to cut it later. Because . . .

Implied Scenes and Pacing

You don't have to show every scene in the story. An implied scene is one you don't film at all, but it's obvious that the scene happened off screen.

Back to that lunch. We're in a living room. A character says, "I've always wanted to try calamari." Cut to: the plate of calamari being placed in front of the character in a restaurant. "Your squid, sir." The character tries to hide his squirmy face. He's having second thoughts.

The exit and entrance are trimmed because we've moved from interaction to interaction. In so doing, the jump to the restaurant created a collection of implied scenes leaving the first building and traveling to the restaurant. We make the connection in our brains. The travel happened. We don't need to see it. It's implied.

Advancing so quickly from interesting bit to interesting bit keeps the pace of the story brisk. A brisk pace works especially well for action and comedy. Lingering in a scene, savoring all its parts and filming scenes that could have been implied, slows down the story. Then again, maybe a lyrical pace might suit the tone of your story.

Beyond implied scenes, pacing also exists within a scene and within a shot. In movies, see how car chases and fight scenes are constructed. There are lots of short, often blurry shots that don't show the entire movement. Visually fast, they cut from movement to movement and keep the audience a little disoriented.

An ambling walk in the park between two people too shy to talk to each other would not work well with that kind of fast pacing. In this case, plan to linger in the scene and moment. Let the camera roll and use longer takes. The action can play out in the shot instead of cutting from angle to angle. Enjoy the scenery as the characters do.

What scenes in your movie need fast pacing vs. slow? You have the power to choose. Any scenes that are interesting enough but don't have story meaning? Make them implied.

Sequences that Reveal Meaning

There also are cases where the scene is part of a sequence (a series of scenes) that doesn't reveal its story meaning until the sequence is complete.

Scene One: the pop star spies enter a garden shed. It's a short scene and not much seems to happen, but it's odd. Why a shed? The audience's curiosity is piqued.

Scene Two: the pop star spies walk down a set of stairs. Clues are unfolding scene by scene.

Scene Three: the pop star spies enter the spy manager's office. The "punch line" is revealed and the audience connects that the spy manager's office is underground. The sequence tells us so. As for story meaning? We know now that these spies are super-secret. They are the elite of the spy world and will be the right ones to track down the unusual Middle C thief . . . which also connects the sequence to the coming climactic scene between hero and villain. That's a lot of story meaning for a short sequence!

What sequences are in your movie? Might you need one to set up connections for a visual joke (like the underground office)?

The Power of Juxtaposition

Juxtaposition. Great word, isn't it? It's a fancy word for putting two things together side-by-side to create an effect. Juxtaposition is a powerful friend, especially of the Editor.

Want to know a secret? Moving pictures (aka movies) don't actually move at all. They are a series of still photos that our eyes watch in quick succession. Our brain fills in the gaps, linking the slightly different photos and telling us that the images must be moving.

Juxtaposition works the same way. Place two scenes next to each other and the viewer will try to find a connection between the scenes. When it works well, the reaction is an emotional response.

Look at these three scenarios:

Write! Shoot! Edit! JUXTAPOSITION SCENARIOS		
Scenario A	**Scenario B**	**Scenario C**
Scene 1 Everyone has a pet except the hero. He bravely says he doesn't need a pet because everyone else has one. His smile is forced.	The friend informs the hero that a certain criminal was just released from jail. Since the hero was responsible for the criminal being caught at the pet store, isn't the hero nervous about going to work (at the pet store)? The hero puts on a brave face but admits he has to go to work.	The hero and his spouse banter about buying a pet. The spouse wants one. He doesn't. They decide on a bet, the winner also winning the pet issue. The hero is superbly confident that the house, the car and favorite chair will be completely and entirely pet-free.
Scene 2 The hero looks in the pet store window, but doesn't go inside.	The hero looks in the pet store window, but doesn't go inside.	The hero looks in the pet store window, but doesn't go inside.
Result **Sadness (poignancy).** Feel it? He wants a pet after all, doesn't he?	**Suspense.** Feel a little worried for him this time?	**Comedy.** Do you feel a little of his resignation? Want to laugh at his arrogance?

Figure 9. Juxtaposition in three scenarios.

1 + 1 = 3. This is the power of juxtaposition. Scene plus scene equals two scenes plus a meaning. Scene 2 is the same for each scenario. We don't know how to react to it—we don't know the scene's meaning—until we've seen the previous scene placed next to it. Which scene precedes it forces us to make very different conclusions.

Connecting with Contrast and Symmetry

We also make connections within the frame. These connections can make for emotional reactions too.

A character in despair, but unable to cry, stands under an umbrella with rain falling all around. There is symmetry between image and emotion. The rain is the tears that the character can't cry. We see it. We feel it.

Another character in despair, but unable to cry, stands morose at a crowded, lively party. The character is visually alone amid a crowd. The contrast between the character's emotion and the upbeat party makes us keenly aware of the emotional distress, especially if the camera is locked on the character, not moving around the lively surroundings.

These examples show contrast and symmetry within the frame. Use it between shots and scenes, too. A messy room, for example, will look messier if the preceding or next shot is of a particularly clean and tidy location. But then, you know that about your bedroom and the rest of your home already, don't you?

Experiment with contrast and symmetry in your movie. Which approach touches you more or provides the reaction you intend?

No Telepathy Here (Show, Don't Think)

Another secret: there is no telepathy in movies. Ya think? Let me explain. Pick up one of your favorite books and read a passage. Chances are the text will include what the character is thinking as well as doing. You can't do that in the movies. You can only see (the picture) and hear (the sound).

Search your script for action descriptions that represent thoughts. Seek out phrases like: "He thinks about what they said yesterday," or "She remembers when . . ." or "They knew that . . ." Such phrases are off-screen thoughts. You can't physically shoot them. Come up with a plan to handle them before filming. Here's what you can do with a screen thought:

Remove it: Your first option is to remove the thought entirely. If it's not critical to the story, strike it from the script. You probably don't need it. But if you do (and I mean really do), rewrite the script passage to convert the thought into one of the following:

Action: Acting out thoughts is a viable option. For example: the hero picks up a photo, then looks sad or pensive. The thought is now generic (though clearly related to the photo). We focus instead on the emotion. Be warned that the more specific the thought, the more difficult it is for new and non-actors to effectively perform the emotional thought on screen.

Dialogue: If the thought can be voiced in some way, dialogue is an option. Don't label the thought specifically. Talk around it. The subtle approach is more human. Instead of "I remember when they left. I was really sad then too, so I stopped playing the game," use "I don't play that game anymore. Not since . . . a while now." We understand the character was so sad at the event, she couldn't even speak the words.

Narration or Voice-Over: Narration introduces a new character or a new perspective of the on-screen character. Choose this option if you plan on a stylistic change to the entire movie. Too much narration slows the story down as we listen to the narrator make comment after comment.

Subtitles: Subtitles are traditionally used for translating on-screen dialogue that's in a different language, but you could use it to label specific thoughts. It's a more technical option and, again, would be a stylistic choice that affects the entire movie. They're time-consuming to create. On set you need to plan the timing of the scene to include the subtitle thought (time for the audience to read it), and in postproduction . . . well, there's an added layer of work laying down the words.

Flashbacks: While we're talking about pricey options, you could add a scene that flashes back to the moment of the thought in the past. Flashbacks interrupt the flow of the story and slow the forward momentum, but they can also make it very clear about what the character is thinking in the present.

There are no rules about how short or long a flash-back can be, but they are expensive in both time and money. Think a new location and/or lighting, more performers, costume changes, props, sets and the time to shoot the flashback scene.

Now, I'm not saying characters can't think on screen. Far from it. They better think! As a Director, consider how you are going to portray that dimension of thought using only picture and sound.

Dimensions in Sound

I can't avoid talking about "sound" in a chapter about visual storytelling! Picture, you see, is only half the story. Watch a movie with the soundtrack turned off and you'll understand.

Take music, for example. By itself, music touches our emotions, so it's no wonder that movies use it in soundtracks all the time. In real life, music never swells as you walk into a classroom . . . but in a movie it can! Use contrast or symmetry between picture and sound to select appropriate music for the scene. If the choice is right, you'll feel the scene as well as see it.

Sound effects can do double duty, too. Just as rain can stand in for tears, a car horn can stand in for a scream. A character is frightened and opens his mouth to scream but there is no sound yet.

Cut to: A traffic jam and someone leaning on the car horn. Yes, it's still a car horn, but thanks to juxtaposition, we connect the horn to the scream.

Finally, what if you were to hear a scene but not see it? A shot of an abandoned cell phone on the kitchen table and voice in the background: "I got my phone, really I do!" and then hear the characters exit. The camera is focused on the cell phone and the soundtrack on the dialogue—because that's where the story is visually (with the phone) and audibly (at the door).

Decode these visual storytelling concepts in the next movie you watch. Experiment with a few of them yourself. Try something new with each movie. It's the language of the movies.

If you are following the path of Writer, go to
Chapter Eleven: Your Premiere and Future (page 135).

If you are following the path of Director, go to
Chapter Four: Prepping the Script for the Shoot (page 38).

If you are following the path of Editor, go to
Chapter Six: Preproduction: Designing the Shoot (page 59).

Chapter Six

Preproduction – Designing the Shoot

The script's in your hand. You have a place to shoot. Friends and family are on board. You're so ready! Right? Wrong.

Okay, you're not wrong. You do need to tap into everything and everyone around you to shoot the movie. But, no good play goes on without previous rehearsal. No competition is won without previous practice. No shoot is successful without preproduction ("prep"). So turn your mind to movie making before the camera rolls. It's actually a lot of fun pulling all the elements together.

Casting, Crewing and Equipping Up

Making a movie is a team sport. A professional production can have anywhere from 50 to well over 150 people on set on a given production day. For first movies, let's scale that number down to reality. Who of your friends and family can commit to the shoot? I mean *really* commit. You can't afford a cast or crew who won't show up because they have something better to do that day. The committed folk will determine your maximum cast and crew size.

CASTING UP

Start with populating the cast. You need them on screen or the movie doesn't happen. For some of the smaller parts, the cast may be able (and want) to double up as crew members.

Chances are you won't be holding auditions to choose who you want to play each role. Instead, you'll be casting from people you already know and coordinating their availability. Consequently, the production schedule and cast list end up being assembled and modified at the same time. Your first choice person is not available for the shoot? Maybe he's available for a smaller role. Be flexible. You may even need to revise the script to customize a role from, say, a teen girl (one of your friends) to an adult male (your parent) due to availability.

CREWING UP

Rest assured that at total bare bones minimum, it's possible to shoot with a Director-DOP (you), and an on-set Production (and Continuity) Assistant. Possible, but even at that level it's better to have at least one more. Five is a nice number to divvy up the roles and activities and keep the shoot small.

1. **Director/Camera (you)**

2. **Art**

3. **Lighting**

4. **Sound**

5. **Continuity**

If you have too many crew, you need more time to communicate your creative vision and shooting plan, which leads to more overall complexity and prep time.

Because it's your movie, in prep you'll be responsible for everything: finding the locations; choosing the costumes (with the cast); gathering props and decorations for the set; designing a shot list; planning for food and transportation during the shoot; conducting any screen tests you deem necessary or useful; and raising and monitoring the money to be spent. Many of these jobs take more than one person, so tap into your network to share the load. Prep is the opportunity to ignite excited anticipation among the crew. Everyone needs to help out beyond their job title.

On the shoot day, as Director, you will direct the cast and operate the camera. You will also take care of numerous other roles beyond your title: liaising with the location owner; decorating the set; providing the props; ensuring cast is in the correct costumes; and checking that sound is recorded effectively.

No less important than you during the shoot, the Production Assistant(s) can take care of: setting up lights or holding reflectors; helping to dress the set; standing in for lighting or sound tests; positioning the microphone; coordinating the food you already arranged; and basically helping wherever help is needed. If you have a crew that's dedicated for the entire shoot (rather than available on a day-to-day basis), delegate them some of your responsibilities. Let them learn alongside you.

There is one more critical person on set: the Continuity Supervisor. This person is the Editor's representative ("rep"). The job is to ensure that the scenes and shots captured will be sufficient and useful in the editing room. If you are not the Editor, have the Editor play this role on set. If you are the Editor, choose someone who wants to help with editing or someone who has a keen eye for detail and paperwork.

As for official job titles, keep it simple. Yes, the only person in the art department is technically the art director, but some people shy away if the title is too fancy, perceiving the shoot could be a long-term, high-commitment activity. Others focus on securing a fancy job title without doing any of the work to earn it. In cases like these, call everyone a Production Assistant (PA). Customize screen credits later.

EQUIPPING UP

When evaluating camera equipment options, consider what it takes to edit your movie. Your camera (be it a dedicated video camera, GoPro or smart phone) needs to create an output file that the editing software can read and manipulate. The higher picture resolution the better because digital standards increase over time and you want your movie to be watchable years from now. Definitely place the camera on a tripod for stability. Shaky images are fine for well-planned action sequences, but for the entire duration of a film, they inspire nausea. Ugh!

As for the editing software, use one that lets you work with two dialogue tracks and at least two or three sound effects and music tracks. Professional features may use hundreds of tracks of sound to craft their soundscape, so four or five really isn't many. You'll welcome the flexibility of multiple tracks in the editing room.

Once you choose and have access to camera and editing software, shoot a quick test to be sure you can capture, transfer and edit the image.

If you shoot indoors, expect to need lights and the ability to place them so they effectively area-light the scene. Household lamps cast an orange glow and—because they show up in the shot—create light flares in the frame. The hardware store sells inexpensive clamp-on scoop lights (two should suffice) plus any extension cords you'll need. Choose a bright "daylight," "cool white" or "all-spectrum" bulb (in a 100-watt equivalent) to counteract the orange glow and make inside images look normal. To see lamps turned on in the shot, use low-wattage equivalent bulbs in the lamp itself to minimize flare, then rely on off-screen lights to illuminate the scene. If you can afford them, get two grip stands from a photography store, which will allow you to place the scoop lights pretty much anywhere and at any height. If you can't afford the stands, you'll have to resort to clipping lights to book-shelves and other tall furnishings in the room.

For shooting outdoors, there is no need for lights (unless you plan tricky night shots). Instead, the challenge is to soften the shadows from strong sunlight. A reflector from a photography store or white foam core from a stationery store will do the job. Once you see how effective it is, you'll end up using it indoors too.

Don't forget sound. For your camera/editing test, go outside. Find out how quickly sound dissipates out there and how a slight breeze roars on the soundtrack. An external microphone (separate from the camera) close to the speaking performers will dramatically increase the quality of your overall sound. Admittedly, with an external mike, you'll need someone dedicated to holding it in position . . . and holding it very still, because moving a microphone also causes unwanted noise.

ABOUT LEADING PEOPLE

It's your movie. You are the leader of the shoot. A good leader brings on board the right people and lets them do their job. When offered, listen to the team's point of view (and I really do mean listen). Don't be too proud to hear and then toss a good idea just because it's not yours. Your attitude will establish the tone and mood of the shoot. It takes time to listen and include people. Though time is always rushed on a shoot, time spent managing people is well spent. It builds team bonding and respect.

Camera and Lighting Essentials

As the Writer uses a pen or keyboard to craft story, the Director crafts story with a camera by intentionally including and excluding information in the frame. The eye is drawn to light and movement. With that knowledge alone you can control where the audience looks in the picture frame. The question is, where do you want them to look?

FRAMING AND THE RULE OF THIRDS

Practice framing a person in the shot using a still camera. Chances are you'll gravitate to framing the subject in the middle where auto-focus kicks in and takes care of picture clarity for you.

Do you have a little space above the head? Yes? Good. That's called "head room." If you don't have it, the

frame will feel claustrophobic. The eye will be drawn
to watch the movement of that head partly in and
partly out of frame. Give a little room. Free us up to
focus on the person's eyes.

Now, have the person in the shot look over your right
shoulder at an imaginary person beside and behind
you. This framing simulates a scene between two
people. If the subject stays in the center of the frame,
it's a little jarring to cut from Person 1 to Person 2 in
the editing room. The two people will be sharing the
same frame space (the middle). Instead, re-frame the
person to be slightly to the left in the picture frame.
See how you have more empty space in front of the
person now? That's call "leading space." The audience
will follow Person 1's eye line to the leading space
and so when you cut to Person 2 looking the opposite
direction on the right side of the frame, the cut will
feel natural.

This off-center framing is used nearly all the time, not
just for conversations. It's called the "Rule of Thirds."
Yup. Another "three." (See Figure 10.) Draw an imaginary grid like tic tac toe in your camera frame: three
across and three up and down. Place the center of
attention at one of the four intersection points. Looks
nicer than framed dead center, doesn't it? If you have
trouble with auto-focus registering where the subject
is, read your camera's manual to find a way to over-
ride or aim the auto-focus.

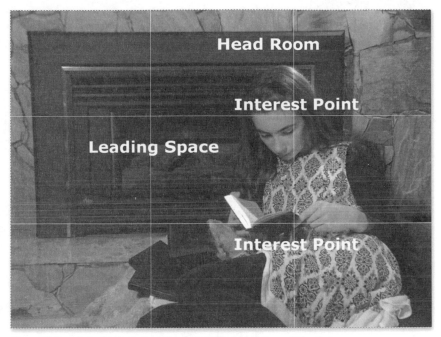

Head Room

Interest Point

Leading Space

Interest Point

Figure 10. Framing with the Rule of Thirds, including head room and leading space.

Sometimes you want to frame off-center for other
reasons. Do you plan to superimpose a title over the
shot? Leave sufficient blank frame space that's not
too visually busy so you can clearly read the titles
when they're added in post.

AXIS OF ACTION

The Editor is most affected by axis of action, but it's
the shooting crew that has to master it on set. Sports
is the best way of explaining the concept.

When you go to a football game, you sit on one side of
the field and know which team is playing left to right
and which team is playing right to left. The "axis of

Figure 11. Axis of Action—Camera A and B can intercut, but Camera C cannot because it crossed the axis.

action" is an imaginary line that travels down the middle of the field, keeping the team's orientation for you and for sports camera coverage.

Do the same thing on set: keep the camera on one side of the axis of action. The axis is the imaginary line that travels between characters in a scene. If you break axis, a character will "pop" over to the wrong side of the picture frame and the viewer will be disoriented. (See Figure 11.)

Axis is relatively easy to identify when you have two static people in a scene. It becomes more difficult when you add movement or when you add a third or fourth person. For complex scenes, it's best to map out a floor plan of the scene (really!), pencil in the axis and plan the camera positions. If there's one angle you're really not sure about, have the performer read the line to off-camera left as well as off-camera right and see which one makes more sense in the editing room.

If you want to cross the axis, do it "legally." You have two options. Include a shot where the camera is on the axis line (the subject is facing directly into the lens or directly away from it). It's a bridge shot from one side of the axis to the other. Alternatively, use camera movement or performer movement in frame to cross the axis during a shot. Remember, though, once you've crossed the axis, you must stay on the other side with all subsequent camera positions until you do a legal cross again.

BEYOND THE HEIGHT OF THE TRIPOD

It's typical with first films to use the camera at the upper height of the tripod or the height of the person operating the camera. Tripods, however, can do so much more. Choose a height that's right for the story. Shooting at eye-height of the cast is a neutral perspective. Shooting from above their eye-line (looking down on them) makes the characters seem insignificant or powerless in the frame. Shooting from below their eye-line (looking up at them) gives them power.

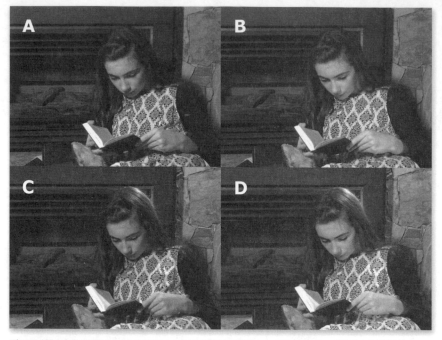

Figure 12. (A) Key light only. (B) Key and fill lights. (C) Key and back lights. (D) 3-point lighting with key, fill and back lights.

Finally, for safety, point one of the tripod legs toward the action. You need room to stand behind the camera, and you don't want the camera to fall forward onto set.

3-POINT AND DIFFUSE AREA LIGHTING

In an ideal world, you'd have three lights on a subject and move them to customize every shot. A key light is the main light on the subject. It's trying to simulate the natural source of light in the room (lamps inside or sun through the window). A softer fill light is aimed from the opposite side to soften shadows created by the key light. Finally, a sharp back light

Figure 13. (A) A reflector can substitute for a fill light, but (B) don't blind your cast with its position.

behind the subject highlights an edge around the head to visually differentiate the subject from the background. (See Figure 12.)

If you only have two lights, use a reflector for the fill light. (See Figure 13.)

For functional lighting of wide shots in your first film, it's okay to go for area lighting. Place the lights above the subjects and off to the side a bit to create a large, diffuse light that illuminates the entire area of action. If a performer stands too close to a light, his image will overexpose (white-out), so place lights after you know where the action will be for the entire scene. Still consider the light source of the room. Can your stronger light simulate the sun from an off-screen window?

When you move in for close-ups, tweak the lighting closer to three-point lighting in order to more clearly see the detail on the performers' faces.

Want to simulate night inside? Don't dim the lights. Instead, manipulate three-point lighting. Remove the fill light and let the key light provide stark shadows while the back light still separates the subject from the background. (See Figure 12C.)

LIGHTING WITH SUN AND SHADE

Outside, put the sun behind the camera whenever possible. It's your key light. For close-ups, use the reflector as a kind of fill light. Since bright sun also causes dark shadows, shoot in the shade for natural diffusion on sunny days. Watch out for that really bright background, though. The eye is drawn to the light. To preview what the camera will see in terms of light and shadow, squint. It's simple and it works.

If you are truly challenged by not having any lights for interiors, see if you can modify the script to move scenes outside. Work with what you have and make it the best it can be. Go more complex next time.

From Scripted Scenes to Shot Lists and Coverage

A scientific fact: moving pictures exist in time as well as in space. You have to design not only what is in the shot, but also how long to keep that shot on the action. It's possible to shoot a scene in one take. Place the camera and have the performers act out the entire scene. Cut. There even have been whole feature films shot in one take (starting with *Timecode* in 2000). Imagine the amount of prep they must have done before the camera rolled! One-take scenes do require a lot of prep and rehearsal. If something is

Figure 14. Framing choices: (A) **Wide shot**. (B) **Medium shot** (based on the subject of interest, not the foreground shoulder). (C) **Close-up**. (D) **Cut-in**.

not quite right during the capture, you have to start all over again. There is no flexibility to edit and speed up the pacing by cutting to an adjacent shot. It's all or nothing (if that's your cuppa tea).

More likely you'll want to work with standard coverage. Shoot the scene in wide shot, then move in for close-ups of each performer (so from a number of different angles). Finally, move in closer again for cut-ins. Cut-ins are details in the shot, like a performer's hand holding a key prop they are talking about. (See Figure 14.)

Cutaways are details that exist outside the shot, like a view through a window to the outside. Cutaways work best when they are triggered by the performer's action in the frame. The performer looks up from the desk to off-screen. Cutaway to the window and its view. The audience connects that the performer has just looked out the window. The Editor on set can recommend useful cut-ins and cutaways to collect for scene pacing in the edit room. If the Editor isn't there, predict and shoot some anyway. Editors love choice.

The good thing about standard coverage is that once you've captured the wide shot, you have the entire scene on film. If you run out of time on set, the wide shot may be your only chance to capture the story "on film." Perhaps it's not the best angle, but you have it and you can finish the movie.

The challenge of standard coverage is that it's tricky for performers. They have to act the scene the same way each time—in wide shot and again in close-up. If they pick up a prop, they have to pick it up at exactly the same time for each shot no matter the angle. If not, the Editor cannot cut from wide to close without exposing the error. A hand that is down in the wide shot but already up in the close-up will pop into frame drawing attention to itself (and away from the story). Here's where the dedicated Continuity Supervisor or Editor-on-Set is invaluable. On a copy of the script, they can pencil in specific actions when they happen in the wide shot, and so prompt performers to repeat those actions when the camera moves in close. As Director, you'll be busy watching the performances and framing for a smooth shot. You'll miss continuity details.

COVER MORE THAN ENOUGH

A final note about coverage. For each shot and angle, shoot a little more action before and after what you intend to use. Create options for your Editor. If, for example, the action ends with the performer opening the door to leave, have the performer stay in character and leave the room entirely. In the editing room, you may wish to extend the shot and you can't unless you filmed a little of what happened after the script says the scene is done.

The same goes for close-ups. Ensure close-ups, cut-ins and cutaways overlap the action in another angle. It's best to cut two shots together on movement (like a character in the process of sitting) instead of before or after the action. In the case of sitting in a chair, cover the act of sitting in both the wide shot and the close-up. The eye is drawn to the movement and will not notice the cut to a new angle, so the edit will appear seamless to the viewer.

To shoot and edit creatively, the camera's presence is invisible. You want the audience to forget they are watching a movie and really get into the story. True movie magic.

Faking it with Doable Special Effects

Speaking of magic, let's talk special effects. Bet the first thing that comes to mind is pricey computer-generated imagery (CGI) animation. Well, there are two kinds of special effects: CGI and physical effects. Many on-set physical effects are quite doable. Movies are about creating illusions. Kick start your imagination and inventiveness to see what you can dream up for your movie. Here are a couple to start you off:

MAGIC (DISAPPEARING OR APPEARING)

How about having someone on screen snap fingers and an object disappears? Position the camera on a tripod and don't move it. Have the performer snap fingers and freeze in place. Run into shot, grab the object and remove it (not touching anything else!). Let the performer unfreeze. In the editing room, edit out the section where you run into the shot and remove the object. If the camera was still and the performer froze well, you'll see the magic. Use the same principle (locked-off camera on a tripod) and you can shoot someone going into a door on the right side of a hallway, but magically coming out of a door on the left in the same hallway.

DOGS THAT TALK

For anything involving pets, you'll only be able to encourage the pet to do what it already does. For dogs, actions could involve sitting, lying down or rolling over. To make a dog talk, a spoonful of peanut butter (if that's in the dog's diet) will supply the necessary mouth movements. For simplicity, add words on the set off-camera. For a bit more work, record lines separately and add them in post.

Cats are less inclined to help you with your movie. Don't they just tolerate us as a species? Well, if you have a cat, you know that already.

LIP SYNC TO MUSIC

There's a little more to playing back a song on a portable device during the shoot and having the performers lip sync to it. Yes, place the microphone near the music to capture the best sound possible. Have the performers practice beforehand so they know the song really well. Roll the camera, then start the action, and finally start the music so you have natural character-like action before the song starts. In post replace the "guide track" music with a higher quality digital copy. Warning: if you use copyrighted music, you will not be allowed to distribute your film publicly in any manner without obtaining prior permission of the musical owners—and there could be several of them depending on the recording you choose.

DAY FOR NIGHT

Shooting during the day and faking it as night is an old Hollywood effect. The trick to doing it well is to use a sunny, cloudless day. Try not to show any sky in the shot (because it will be too bright). Dim the exposure of the camera so the image looks dark, and add a thin blue filter over the lens. Definitely test this trick before committing to it. As an audience we're very used to seeing night-for-night now, so day-for-night is a hard sell to do effectively.

POOR MAN'S PROCESS

Another old Hollywood effect, it's used to fake a moving car. Great name, isn't it? Basically the car stays still and the scenery is moved around it. Add a fan for some wind. Pro shoots use a projection of moving scenery but you could use moving plants, I suppose. Keep the frame tight on the performers so you don't see any non-moving scenery in the background.

GUNS, OR RATHER, GUN ALTERNATIVES

I don't recommend using guns of any type. Fake guns have red on the end of the barrel, so they look obviously fake. For more life-like replicas there's a huge layer of safety protocols you need that involves firearms specialists and officially informing the police and neighbors. Instead, use your imagination. What can you use instead of guns? If its purpose is to threaten, then how else can you do it? Tie up the character to a chair? Use fake handcuffs from a Halloween store? It's a creative industry. Be creative. Imply "gun" without using one.

Figure 15. Faking an arrow shot—backstage. Shot 1: Not shooting the arrow, but aiming at a nearby safety tree, just in case. Shot 3: Twanging the arrow already in place.

Figure 16. Faking an arrow shot—final sequence.

SHOOTING AN ARROW OR THROWING A SPEAR

What if you want to shoot an arrow or throw something like a spear and have it land near the hero? Naturally you can't actually do it safely. Let's take the bow and arrow. To fake it takes three shots. Shot #1: The archer draws the bow but doesn't shoot (and there's a safety surface off screen in case of an accidental release). Shot #2: Swish-pan from somewhere near the archer to somewhere near the hero. A swish pan is when the camera moves side-to-side so fast that the image is totally blurry. With it, you're pretending to follow the arrow mid-flight. Shot #3: The arrow already in its destination near the hero. You can even twang it so that it stops moving during the shot. The hero reacts as if the arrow just landed. Cut the three shots together in post and you have faked an amazingly accurate archery shot. (See figures 15 and 16.)

BLOOD

Halloween shops have fake blood and scars if you want to go there. Be careful that the blood doesn't stain clothing or furnishings. Who wants a surprise cleaning bill at the end of the shoot? As for stage blood recipes, there are plenty available on the Internet (mostly involving corn syrup, red dye and various other ingredients). Still, many movies and computer games simulate death without the need to splatter blood. Know that the more complex you go with effects and stunts, the more people you'll need on set to ensure safety, coordinate the elements, and clean up.

IT'S ALL IN THE REACTION

How about a non-effect? Much can be done by the actor's performance alone. Someone can fall into a trap door in the floor by abruptly dropping out of the shot. Another can mime being electrocuted when touching a fence. Yet another can react to an off-screen event by looking shocked and wince while a series of sound effects (that you'll lay down in post) betray an elaborate off-screen stunt that you can't afford to shoot. Have fun with reaction shots! Often the story—and audience's attention—is in the reaction shot anyway.

What special effects are you dreaming up now? Screen test them. Since you are conducting other camera or lighting tests during prep, double-up by testing effects you have in mind at the same time.

All that You See from Costumes to Props

Back to decorating all that you see: the realm of the art department. Refer to those scene-by-scene script breakdowns you made and the script. How many different costumes do you need for each character to cover the number of script days in the story? Involve the cast in their costume choices, tapping into their wardrobe wherever possible. Stay away from logos on clothing. Sometimes they trigger permissions you have to arrange or purchase. They can distract the viewer's eye from the performances and story.

Secondhand stores are a terrific stop for wardrobe treasures. Once you've assembled an outfit, take a still photo of it and let the cast and Continuity Supervisor ensure the costume is visually duplicated every time it's required on set. I also highly recommend that you—or a dedicated wardrobe crew member—store all costumes and bring them to set. You want the performers remembering their lines and showing up. Free them of the responsibility of remembering continuity details of their costumes.

Makeup and hair? Well, you probably don't need makeup. If you need a little powder to tame the shine on someone's forehead, stay hygienic. Use separate makeup for each performer. Regarding hair, consult with performers to design hair styles that they can take care of for the shoot. Remind them not to cut their hair for the duration of the shoot. Yes, some people will need this obvious reminder.

Props are objects that the performers touch or hold during a scene. They are written in the script and can be anything from a pencil to a sandwich to a test tube to your depiction of the physical representation of Middle C. Like costumes, as you assemble them, store them so the props arrive on set for the necessary scenes. Take still photos of props too, especially if they need to be re-created or rebuilt between shots or takes.

A warning note about food: don't have performers eat on screen. Because of standard coverage and the numerous takes required to get it right, you'll be committing yourself to buying tons of whatever food it is and committing the performers to eating the same thing over and over and over again for the camera.

Imaginary Script, Real Life Locations

Look at the required list of locations. If the script was drafted "story first" you'll probably see locations that look completely unfindable: concert hall, morgue, etc. Have no fear. Identify what is the minimum you have

Figure 17. (A) A shot looking from backstage to onstage using three curtains, but (B) the concert hall setup is actually in a living room.

to see (or hear) to make the location work on screen. Remember you'll be showing the place to the audience via a small viewing port: the camera lens.

Take the pop stars and their benefit concert at the end of the movie. Now, picture looking at the stage from backstage, not from the audience's point of view (it's more cool to be backstage anyway). For the stage, all you need is a large, blank wall (or curtained wall) plus two black curtains in the foreground of the shot obscuring a complete view of the stage. Basically, you're visually hinting that a stage is beyond the black curtains. Now lay in a track of the music, and a sound effects track of enthusiastic fans and you've put the audience there: backstage at the concert. Bet you can find that wall at a local, friendly school or church. (See Figure 17.)

Set dressing is all the rest of the decorations on the set or location that make us believe the space we're in. For backstage, it was the black curtains (and the clips and frame used to hold them in position).

What details will it take to make the real locations you have access to look like the imaginary ones you have in the script? Glassware, test tubes, hoses and clamps can turn a garage into a laboratory. Lots of boxes in an empty room will tell us it's moving day at the house or apartment.

Set decorations are implied, not specified, in the script, so start designing spaces! Photograph the location before you start (as well as when it's dressed) so you can return the location back to starting decor. Leave the location as good as or better than you found it and the owner will be more than happy to allow you to come back for your next film . . . or for re-shoots for this one.

If you are following the path of Director, go to **Chapter Five: Your Visual Storytelling Toolbox (page 46)**.

If you are following the path of Editor, go to **Chapter Eight: Production: The Shoot (Finally!) and Wrap (page 98)**.

Chapter Seven:

Preproduction: Juggling the Logistics

Logistics are all those niggly details that have to be done so that all the right people and all the right equipment show up at the right location at the right time. They're so important, they deserve their own niggly chapter.

Jigsaw Puzzle Scheduling

The shooting schedule. It's quite the juggling act to fit your movie into the busy lives of people and places around you. In your mind's eye, you're already placing set decorations to create the script's imaginary locations. In reality, you need to piece together a shooting schedule so people can commit to a tangible where and when.

HOW MANY DAYS?

Start by identifying the number of days you need to shoot. For first films, you'll probably shoot one location per day, although if the script has a lot of story material at that location, it could be two days at one place. Because you need setup and clean-up time at each space (beyond shooting time), moving from location to location takes a whole lot longer than you think it will. It's not impossible to do a "unit move," it's just time consuming. There are only so many daylight hours and you'll want to be shooting, not moving, when the sun is up. Pro shoots have the luxury of prep and wrap teams who can decorate the set in advance of the shooting crew's arrival, and strike it afterward. You, on the other hand, will be doing it all.

COMBINING SCENES

If the script has a veritable ton of locations, can you combine any? Take this example: Scene 1: a character enters a building. Scene 2: the character meets someone in an office inside the building and they argue. In Scene 1, we learn that the character enters a particular building; however, if in Scene 2, the character enters the room and removes a jacket, we learn the same thing. You don't have to shoot Scene 1 at all! Save yourself the few hours of shooting (prep, shoot and wrap outside the building).

OTHER PEOPLE'S SCHEDULES
Next, you need to fit into other people's schedules . . . within reason. Here's where scheduling feels like putting together a jigsaw puzzle. Chances are you'll be back and forth a bit with locations and people to assemble the parts.

During this process you may find you have to shuffle the cast and crew or bring in a new friend or two to fill in all the roles on your shoot days. Have faith that changes to cast even at this late date will not ruin your movie. It's in moments like these when previously undreamed of opportunities and friendships flourish. Be open to the possibilities.

THE SHOOTING SCHEDULE / CAST AND CREW LIST
Because of their complexity and serious number of people to organize, pro shoots publish a lot of scheduling documentation: production schedule, one-line schedule, shooting schedule, cast list, crew list, contact list, plus—for each day of production—a call sheet. Bit overkill, don't you think? For first films, indeed! You only need one document. Since your schedule is so closely tied to cast/crew and location availability, summarize all the details on one or two pages. Keep it concise. (See Figure 18.)

Write! Shoot! Edit!

First Film Schedule and Cast/Crew List
[Date of Schedule]

Sc.#	Description	D/N	Pages	Cast	Notes
Day 1 – Sunday, [Date] – 1pm to 4pm					
Location – [Address, phone number]					
Sc.4	INT. KITCHEN	D1	2	Dreya, Sue	Burnt cookies
Sc.7	INT. KITCHEN	D2	1	Sue	Dog, Book stack
Day 2 – Saturday, [Date] – 1pm to 3pm (wrapped by 4pm)					
Location – Church [Address, phone number]					
Sc.8	INT. STUDIO	N2	1	Dreya, Fan	Black curtains

(etc)

Cast
Dreya: [Name] – [contact numbers]
Natty: [Name] – [contact numbers]
Fan: [Name] – [contact numbers]

Crew
Director: [Your Name] – [contact numbers]
(etc)

Figure 18. The combined shooting schedule and cast/crew list centralizes critical information.

Notice that the shoot days have nothing to do with the days of the week. You can easily have six non-shoot days between days 1 and 2.

D/N stands for day or night as specified in the script. The number next to the letter identifies which costume change is used for that scene. The number is called the "script day."

When it comes to page counts, pro shoots go by eighths of pages. Forget eighths. Round to the nearest page or half-page.

The cast list can be by name (as shown in Figure 18) or by number—one for each character. For numbers, include a legend at the bottom of the page. If you have room, actual names are better.

For the notes, only list the unique items that are critical to that particular scene, such as special effects, someone's dog, or anything that might make shooting that scene take longer than "normal." Any special safety notes needed for the shoot day? Include them here, too.

As for the cast and crew section, include everyone you plan to grant a screen credit.

Finally, if you want to be even fancier, add a micro-short scene description for each scene on a second line. It makes the document longer, but it's a good memory prompt for each scene, especially if several scenes are at the same script location.

A Nod to the Business Side of the Biz

On one hand there's time (the schedule). On the other hand there's money and permissions (the business). Don't yawn! You think the business side of filmmaking is boring and pointless for first films. I hear you.

Now, let me tell you the minimum that you do need and why.

Act professional enough and people who help make your film will trust you. People who own locations will let you shoot there. Performers will take you seriously and show up. Look too professional, though, and they'll think you have money to pay them. You need the right balance. You need a nod to the business.

WRITTEN PERMISSIONS (AKA WHO OWNS WHAT?)
It's clear you own the script (assuming that you wrote it alone). Think you own the movie, too? Well, you sort of do and sort of don't. The performers, for example, may agree to act in your movie, but technically they still own their own image even after it's captured on screen. They have a say as to how their filmed image is used and where it is shown after completion. Owners of locations, businesses, logos and music have similar rights. So, too, do cowriters of the script. As mentioned earlier, making a movie is a team sport.

Because of these shared "usage rights," it's good to collect written permissions from people who participate. Clarify three things: what you expect of them; what they can expect of you; and what you intend to do with the movie after completion.

Written agreements for first films don't have to be formal with lots of legalese. Don't try to be a lawyer.

NOTE: This template is not legal advice.

[Date]

Dear [Performer name],

Thanks for agreeing to play [Name of role] in my movie, which is currently called: [Movie title]. You will receive a digital or DVD copy of the movie when it's done. Because it's a home video shot with friends and family, the movie is not intended to be shown publicly or shared on social media. Please do the same (don't show it publicly or share it on social media).

Thanks,

[Your name]

[Your address, email and phone numbers]

Please respond to this email that you agree.

Also please confirm this information is correct:

Your name (as you want to see it on the credits): [Performer Name]

Your address: [Their address]

Your email: [Their email address]

Your phone number: [Their phone number]

Figure 19. An informal performer email agreement.

For performers, you could try an email with wording such as in Figure 19.

This simple permission does triple-duty, clarifying the agreement, giving you the correct spelling of the name for the credits, and supplying you with contact information for your cast/crew list and schedule.

For a location—after agreeing to the where, when, and who details—follow up with an email to summarize

[Date]

[Name of Location Owner]
[Owner's address, email and phone numbers]

Dear [Location Owner name],

Thanks for letting me film some of my movie at your place: [Address or description of location]. You have assured me that you have the right to give me this permission.

As I mentioned, it's a home movie being made with family and friends, and it's currently called: [Movie title]. We'll be shooting on [Date] and will arrive at [Time] and plan to be done at [Time]. We understand that we have to be done by [Time] at the very latest.

Because it's a home video, the movie is not intended to be shown publicly or shared on social media. Please let me know if you'd like a digital or DVD copy of the movie when it's done, and if you receive one, please don't show it publicly or share it on social media.

Thanks,

[Your signature]
[Your name]
[Your address, email and phone numbers]

Figure 20. An informal location email agreement.

the verbal agreement. You can use the wording in Figure 20 to inspire your email.

Other information you could include: a short description of the movie (a spy adventure, a mystery, etc.) plus a description of the scene you're shooting there; the arrangements for key access; and any other detail that directly affects your shoot day. Be brief but be clear.

Another note about locations: renters are not the location owners. They don't have the right to let you shoot there. Track down the actual owner before the owner finds out about your shoot after the fact.

Finally, collect all your written permissions into a folder and keep them as long as you keep the movie. It could be years and years, so think of a good, long-term place to store it.

INSURANCE

With first films, you won't be able to afford insurance. Pro shoots buy policies to cover equipment, cast and crew (from potential injury), locations, and various other unintentional infringements of rights. At your age, it's unlikely that anyone will sue you if something goes horribly wrong. Instead, they will sue anyone who has money around you: your parents, the location owners, the parents of performers. The message here is the advice you've heard since kindergarten: be safe, play nice. Do so and "nice" will come back to you.

THE MONEY IT TAKES

How much does it cost to shoot a first film? Even if you say you're going to make the movie for free, it will cost something. It's easy to overspend if you don't have a plan and don't monitor costs. No one wants to stop production because the money ran out. Draft a simple budget plan. Figure 21 is a sample budget to start with and customize.

Write! Shoot! Edit!

First Film Sample Budget

Budget assumptions:
4 shoot days, 5 crew (including you), 6 cast (but no more than 3 on any given day), 3 locations.

CREW	$0	All volunteers; give copy of finished movie.
CAST	$0	All volunteers; give copy of finished movie.
LOCATIONS	$0	All free access; give copy of finished movie.
OFFICE	$0	Existing computer and email. Scrounge for highlighters and pencils and masking tape.
PHOTOCOPIES	$30	For black ink; print at least 20 copies of script for cast/crew, plus schedule/crew list.
CAMERA	$0	Existing camera. Borrow tripod.
LIGHTING	$135	Buy reflector ($25), 2 clamp lights ($20/ea), 2 light stands ($35/ea). Borrow extension cords.
SOUND	$0	Existing microphone.
EXPENDABLES	$20	2 full spectrum bulbs ($10/ea). Scrounge for other one-use items (like duct tape, batteries) for camera/lighting/sound.
ART SUPPLIES	$30	Scrounge for set decorations, props and costumes. Buy some from secondhand stores.
CRAFT SERVICE	$120	Food/snacks for 4 days x $30/day (up to 8 people) because everyone is there for free. Include garbage/recycling supplies.
CONTINUITY PIX	$0	Existing camera.
EDIT SOFTWARE	$60	Purchase shareware to have tech support and plan to use for future films anyway.
MUSIC/SOUND FX	$0	Plan music/sound effects available for free.
POST STORAGE	$0	Existing external hard drive (need because video files are big).
FINISHING	$40	At least 20 copies of finished movie (DVD and/or flash drive).
TOTAL =	**$435**	

Second Film Sample Budget

Same details and budget as the first one, but lighting equipment and editing software are previously purchased:

TOTAL =	**$240**

Figure 21. A sample budget for two first films.

Looks like a lot of money, doesn't it? Well, every movie is different. That's why I included a second budget at the same time. Bet you can already see places where you can save money for your film. Might your parents donate the food?

Notice that each budget number is justified by a written explanation. Budget numbers don't exist in a vacuum. Explain each one.

Free items are also included so that you know just how much people are contributing. In this particular example, there is access to some equipment, but lighting equipment and post software are planned purchases. Your situation could be different.

Estimate the costs of your movie, then enlist family to help fund it. With a budget that clearly explains how much you need and why, they'll be more inclined to help. They may even have ideas on sources to help you reduce costs further.

Your Prep Survival Checklist

You're almost there! This close to production it's a comfort to have a checklist to double-check that you have what you need when the camera rolls. Pull out your pencils and start checking. (See Figure 22.)

Write! Shoot! Edit!
First Film "Prep Survival" Checklist

The Story
☐ **SCRIPT** - copies for everyone, plus a spare for the shoot day

The Plan
☐ **SHOT LIST** – as notes and/or storyboard drawings in a separate document or annotated on your script

☐ **SCHEDULE / CAST AND CREW LIST** – copies for everyone, plus a spare for the shoot day

☐ **CONTINUITY** – copy of the script, pencil, continuity photos from prep for costumes/props

People
☐ **CREW** – each one with latest script, schedule/cast/crew list, plus written permission done

☐ **CAST** – same notes as for crew, but do they also have their costumes and know what to do with their hair?

Equipment
☐ **EQUPMENT FOR THE SHOOT** – camera, tripod, reflector, lighting and stands, microphone

☐ **EQUIPMENT FOR EDITING** – computer, digital storage, software (tested from camera to output file)

Art supplies
☐ **ART SUPPLIES** – Costumes, makeup, props, set decorations, special effects supplies – key items photographed and labeled for each scene to re-create them identically each time

Locations and logistics
☐ **LOCATIONS** – permissions in hand from owners; balloons and string to use as signage for hard-to-find locations and supplies to remove any garbage you generate

☐ **TRANSPORTATION** – can cast and crew make it to the locations?

☐ **FOOD AND SNACKS** (a.k.a. "CRAFT SERVICE") – what snacks do you have and who is supplying/serving them? If you schedule to shoot over a meal break, you must feed the people. They are doing you a favor being part of your movie, plus you don't want to hear rumbling stomachs on screen. If you shoot over too many lunch breaks, watch the production budget soar.

Figure 22. A checklist to help you survive the niggly details of preproduction (prep).

Okay, you're there. You have the production plan. You've tested it. You know how much it's going to cost. Time to roll that camera.

 Since you're following the path of Director, continue on!

Chapter Eight:

Production - The Shoot (Finally!) and Wrap

Roll camera! Now that you're actually shooting, you won't want to spend much time reading a book. I'll try to keep this chapter short so you can get on with it, be it shooting or editing.

There's a surreal sense of "is this it?" on the first day of principal photography (the shoot). The movie doesn't look like a script anymore and it's not supposed to. It's time for Wild Inventor to step back while Dr. Structure and Nitpicky take the lead during the shoot. You'll consult Wild Inventor to help you out of unforeseen events, but more on those later. Let's go through the shoot day structure in order to capture all necessary scenes in what limited time you have. It's amazing how quickly time slips away during the shoot.

Scenes, Shots, Setups, Takes and Slates

Vocab recap! . . . because you want to sound like a pro on set.

The script is divided into scenes. Typically a scene break happens when there is a change in time or space in the story. A scene break becomes obvious on set, because you have to physically move to a new location or stop filming while the cast changes costumes.

A shot is a camera angle on the scene. It could be a wide shot showing the whole room, a close-up showing only one of the characters, or a cut-in (or insert) showing a small detail. A shot does not have to capture the action of the entire scene, but you should overlap action between shots so the Editor has choices where to make the cut in the editing room.

A setup is the placement of camera and lighting equipment in order to capture a shot. Typically there is one setup per shot, but if you capture a wide shot, then zoom in and capture a close-up without physically moving the camera; then you have more than one shot for that setup.

A take is one attempt to capture a shot. You may find you need four or more takes before you're happy with the performance, camera operation, sound and lighting quality. Note that non-actors tend to fade in their performances after the third take. No surprise, really. Add together the number of shots plus takes you need to capture the scene. That's a lot of repeat performances!

The slate is that black-with-stripes Hollywood clapboard that you've probably seen on behind-the-scenes documentaries. On the blackboard, the movie name, scene, shot and take numbers are written so the Editor can identify the shot in postproduction. When the slate is clapped shut at the start of a scene, it's the visual and audio identifier for the Editor to sync picture with sound. Since you'll be recording picture and sound together, you won't need to "clap," but do make a slate to visually identify the scene, shot, and take. You can go as simple as a piece of paper and marker, or add to the fun by sourcing a real-looking slate at a party supply store and tape on the scene, shot, and take information.

Who Says What? (Shoot Day Structure)

Now that you're talking and looking like a pro, here's how to structure each shot so that everyone knows and trusts that you are in charge. There's a cycle of four activities to do for every shot. Start with an announcement:

"First we're going to block out the action of the scene."

I. **BLOCK**—Even before you place the camera, walk through the scene with the performers. Imagine where you'll place the camera (or have it roughly in place to capture the wide shot). There is no serious acting, yet. The performers can still hold their scripts. Identify where the performers need to be and move during the scene. Use masking tape to mark key stopping points on the floor. If you're outside, use pebbles. Work with the performers to modify your planned "blocking" if the movement doesn't seem natural. Test camera position (and camera movement, if any). By the end of blocking, the camera should be in its position for the shot. Announce something like:

"That's good for blocking, thank you. Next we're going to light the set."

2. **LIGHT**—Now the cast and crew know how the scene is going to play out, it's time to light the set. If needed, release the cast to finish dressing in costume or to practice lines. If already dressed, have them assist lighting by standing in those key stopping points. Expect to spend a bit of time lighting the wide shot. When you move in for close-ups, you may only need to tweak the lights to make it work. Don't forget to practice placing the microphone—without its casting shadows within the framed shot—while you're lighting. Consider safety: Cover cords and cables on the floor with mats. For lights, use extension cords long enough to wrap gently around light stands (or similar) to prevent accidents. Make hazard-spotting a game, if you like, so that everyone is part of making a safe set. When lighting is ready, announce something like:

"We're good for lighting, thank you. Next we're going to rehearse and shoot the scene."

3. REHEARSE—Although camera, lights, and cast are ready, you need to run through the shot (entire scene, if possible). The cast needs to practice the scene without script in hand. The crew needs to practice with the equipment (like placing the microphone), and you need to practice operating the camera. Frame and follow the action as if you were filming it. The tricky bit now is to shoot before the cast fades from repeated performances, and after you and crew have had enough practice to be smooth technically. When you think you're ready, announce:

"That's great, thank you. We're going to shoot the next one."

4. SHOOT—First, assess that each crew member is ready to shoot. Is the slate marked and clearly in frame so it will be legible in post? Is the Continuity Supervisor ready to take notes? Is the mike in position? Are cast at first positions? Announce:

"Roll camera!" and start the camera.

This announcement is for the benefit of both cast and crew. If the set is in a public place where you have crew stopping the odd person from passing by during the shot, the announcement tells crew when to stop people. Especially for noisy and outside sets, crew can relay this announcement to the far edges of your set by saying, "We're rolling!"

Nod to the person holding the slate or say, "Slate."

In response, that person reads the information: "Scene 4, Shot 1, Take 1." and then removes the slate from the frame. When the frame is clear and ready, call:

"Action!"

This word is primarily for the benefit of the cast. Make sure the cast waits a short beat before actually starting their performance. You don't want your word "action" to overlap any of their lines. Though you may need to yell the command if it's a wide shot in the noisy outdoors, you can speak the word softly when you're indoors, close, and all is quiet.

While capturing the shot, evaluate the performances, your camera moves, and check that the microphone doesn't sneak into the shot. Sounds busy, doesn't it? A lot is going on inside that camera frame. You'll be happy to have someone else jot down the continuity notes for editing. After the action is completed, wait a short beat, then call:

"Cut! Thank you," and then stop the camera.

Make this ending announcement clear for both cast and crew. It releases the set hush, and signifies crew to allow any patient passersby to continue about their way.

Now it's time to make a decision if you need another take or you're ready to move on to the next setup. Even if the first take is terrific, capture a "safety" (Take 2) in case you didn't see something in the frame during filming that you'll want to remove later.

Decision made, announce to the cast and crew what's next:

"Back to first positions, please. We'll shoot one more for safety." or "That's it for this setup. We'll move the camera and move in for close-ups."

Then you're back to blocking again. When you move in close, it's true that the scene's movement is already blocked. For blocking this time around, you just need to identify which part of the scene will be covered, and place the camera to see if the lights need tweaking. So, yes, repeat all four steps each time:

block, light, rehearse and shoot

Directing Actors, Leading Crew

Can't wait to give directions to friends, parents and adults? The spotlight is on you!

Yes, you'll be giving a lot of directions. Not orders. Being a leader is more about inspiring people to do their best than it is about lording it over them how superior you think you are.

When it comes to the cast, put yourself in their shoes for a moment. They're performing the story out of order. It's not easy. Help by reminding them what happened in the story before this scene and what comes later. Talk with (not to) them about the performance. Include their opinions with yours to help them succeed. They are not there to imitate the performance in your mind's eye. They become the characters, and will be a little different from what you imagined in prep. Be sympathetic, too. The cast stands before the camera. Everything they say and do is recorded. It's very similar to (and more permanent than) public speaking. Chances are some of them are more nervous than you are.

When it comes to the crew, the organization you did in prep will inspire the crew to treat you as the leader. You have a shooting plan: shooting schedule, shot list and budget. Share the plan with the crew. On set, use the block-light-rehearse-shoot structure for a comfortable, predictable routine.

If you're always making it up as you go along, their trust wavers and the time you spend thinking about what to do next will slow the shoot day down to a painful slog. Crew may start to find excuses not to show up for subsequent days.

Rather than issuing orders, ask people to do things. Listen to their ideas. You may not use many of them, but take a moment to really listen and think about it. Be thankful, and then make a decision. A movie is creative collaboration (not a majority-wins democracy). By really listening, the crew will feel respected and reciprocate by respecting you. Besides that, you're going to need their ideas when the unforeseen happens.

Handling the Unforeseen

Imagine you planned to shoot outside at the beach on a sunny day, but the shoot day rolls around and rain is bucketing down.

Imagine showing up at the church basement location to find out that though they promised you 4 hours, there's another community group coming in for a meeting in 2 hours.

Imagine a cast member has a fender bender with his parent's car while on your set and you may no longer use the car or cast member for the shoot.

The unforeseen. It happens.

For the beach, perhaps you can rewrite the scene on the fly and bring in umbrellas, or move the scene to another location. For the church, if there is no negotiating the shared space (meetings don't like to be quiet during a take), you may need to simplify coverage and be out in 2 hours. Alternatively, you might be able to reschedule to another date and time. For the car, what would you do?

1. **Be organized and responsible (with shot list, shooting schedule, and budget).**

2. **Know your story and be flexible. You may need to rewrite quickly.**

3. **Finally, think fast! In order to successfully rewrite or change coverage on the day, you have to already know which scenes and actions are**

important to tell the story. Re-read Chapter Five on visualizing story and be re-inspired by the concepts. It's unforeseen times like these that will test how much preparation you did, and therefore, how well you know the script and story.

As for the car incident, it happened to me on the first day of shooting. I so wanted to quit, but didn't. I met with the parents to discuss the situation. The cast member was allowed to continue, but not the car. We re-wrote the scene without the car, finished the film, were written up in the paper (a great article about the movie, not the car), and because of the film, the two leads met, later married and had two fabulous kids. Who'd've thought? Now that was truly unforeseen!

Continuity: The Editor's Rep on Set

It's invisible if it's well done: continuity. A truly backstage and unsung job, the Continuity Supervisor makes critical notes for the Editor, ensures the script is entirely shot, and catches continuity errors on set before they are captured by the camera.

CONTINUITY FOR COSTUMES, PROPS AND SETS

Refer to the costume photos taken in prep to ensure that the cast outfits match the design. You may shoot two scenes a day or weeks apart, but if the same cast shows up in both those scenes when cut together in post, their outfits better match perfectly in both scenes. For necklaces, always put the clasp at the back of the neck. If there's a collar, pay special attention to its position, because being so close to the face, a continuity error on collar position is noticeable.

Still photos are great references. After the set is decorated (or a significant prop is built), grab a picture of it and hang on to it. In post you may need to re-create all or part of the set for a re-shoot.

SCRIPT NOTES AND SHORTHAND

Sit near the camera to approximate the camera's view of the scene. While watching the wide-shot action (presumably the action of the entire scene), make notes on the script of performance actions that will need to be duplicated when the camera moves in close. Actions could be: picking up a prop, standing up or sitting down. Because it all happens so fast, use shorthand for your notes. Arrows, for example, can quickly identify directional movement (up arrow for standing up, down arrow for sitting down).

When the camera actually rolls, mark on the script when the shot starts and stops. Again, use pencil and shorthand, like this:

WS: wide shot
CU: close-up
ECU: extreme close-up
MS: medium shot
2S: two-shot (two characters in the shot)
3S: three-shot (three characters in the shot)
INS: insert shot or cut-in (no character's face in the shot)

At the starting point, put the shot number in a circle and describe the type of shot (WS, CU, ECU, etc). Draw a line through the script until the shot ends. If the dialogue in the script is captured on-camera, use a straight line. If the dialogue is off-screen, use a wavy one. Mark the end of the shot with a dash. (See Figure 23.)

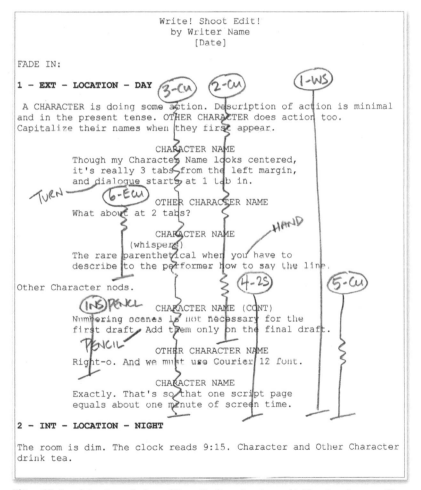

Figure 23. A script page marked up with continuity notes shows significant performer actions and shot coverage.

Notice how, at a glance, you can see which parts of the script have been captured on screen and not?

If the Director is not the Editor, have the Editor play Continuity's role on set. Otherwise, find someone who has great attention to detail.

Wrap it Up

There sure is a lot of wrapping done on set: each shot, location, cast, and finally the shoot. Let Nitpicky speak up with "are you sure?" There are plenty of details to consider before and during wrap (finish and clean up).

WRAP THE SHOT
When you think the shot is done, ask yourself a few questions. Was the performance good? Was the shot in focus? Was camera operation smooth? Was sound clear? Did the shot overlap action with another angle (to give options for editing)? If all's well, move on to the next shot.

WRAP THE LOCATION
Finished shooting at a particular set or location? Capture about 30 seconds of the quiet room with everyone on set and standing still. You're capturing "room tone" (essential white noise) for your soundtrack in post. Every room sounds different, and when you add certain furnishings and breathing

bodies, the sound becomes unique. After room tone, announce that location is wrapped, then remove your stuff, tidy up and, as mentioned before, try to leave it as good or better than you found it. When you use someone's space, your shoot—no matter how small it is—represents you, your cast and crew, as well as your family, and gives a first impression of the industry. Send a thank you note to the owner shortly afterward. On to setup of the next location!

WRAP A CAST MEMBER

Not all the cast will be around for the entire shoot. After the last shot for each one, remember to say thanks. You can even announce that it's the last day for that particular person so the crew can add their voice or applaud. You may still need to shoot for days, but for them it's over and they'll be asking about the date and time of the premiere. Inform them or arrange to send the information as soon as you have it.

WRAP THE SHOOT

If the continuity notes say you've shot everything, it's time to wrap principal photography (the shoot). First up, take a moment to thank cast and crew. Tidy up the last location, leaving it as good or better than you found it. Hand the continuity notes to the Editor, and collect the rest of the scripts for now. Recycle them in post after you know there won't be any re-shoots.

Production may have wound down, but postproduction is just ramping up.

Send thank you notes to all involved. In those notes, report or estimate the premiere date—at which time you'll supply them a copy of the finished movie. They've done a lot to help you make this movie possible. Be grateful.

 If you are following the path of Director, go to
Chapter Eleven: Your Premiere and Future (page 135).

 If you are following the path of Editor, go to
Chapter Ten: The Last Word of Postproduction: Sound and Finishing (page 125).

Chapter Nine:

The Last Word of Postproduction - Picture Post

Think that postproduction starts after production ends? Think sooner.

How Soon Post Really Starts

Day 2 of the shoot is Day 1 of postproduction. Really. Admittedly, if you're both Director and Editor, you won't be doing much editing until after the shoot's done. On pro shoots there are separate teams with sufficient crew to start cutting footage together immediately during the shoot.

Now, since editing can start pretty much at the same time as the shoot, preparing for editing has to start before the camera rolls! During preproduction, test the editing software you plan to use. Cut together a couple of shots and lay in a track of sound or two to test that the workflow is technically seamless from capturing images and sound to outputting a final format. The decisions you made to go with, say, freeware with limited post capabilities—like one or two tracks of sound, or a limited file size—directly affect the Director during principal photography (the shoot). Perhaps the limited post capabilities are attractive because the interface is so easy. Whatever you choose, before camera rolls, know the restrictions placed onto production by your choice in editing software.

Story Crafting (for the Last Time) in the Edit Room

Time to make the final story that's seen on the screen at the end of the day. Until now, the script has been a road map (the script from the writing stage and continuity notes from the shooting stage). What the camera actually captured is the raw material from which you are going to craft the story. The real story. How you assemble the pieces is filled with creative opportunity. Feel free to veer from the script's plan when you see the coverage you have.

Let Wild Inventor see the footage with a fresh and new perspective.

At first, it may be overwhelming to see how much coverage (angles, shots and takes) you have. It's possible the shoot provided 8 to 10 minutes of footage for every final minute of film. For a 12-minute film, that could mean 2 hours of footage. What a lot of choices! Is it possible to pare the material down into a cohesive story? Absolutely.

There are four stages of picture editing to help you through the process: rushes, assembly, rough cut and fine cut.

RUSHES (AND PENCIL EDIT)
The first stage is called the rushes because the coverage from set has been "rushed" to the edit room as fast as possible. The slate is still in every shot, as are the words "action" and "cut." As the Editor, however, you don't have to rush with the rushes. Become really, really familiar with every scene, shot and take.

Upload the video files to computer and watch each take. Watch twice if need be. Make notes on the continuity script (or start a separate edit list) of best performances, moments and takes. If you want, flag bloopers for use in a gag reel.

When you think you know each take by heart, leave the editing room. Really? Yes, really.

Take your script with continuity and editing notes to a place where you find quiet inspiration—be it the park, a bathtub, or a tent made with a chair behind the living room curtain. Okay, the bathtub could prove a bit too soggy.

Invoke Wild Inventor to help you think through the edited movie. Preview it on the imaginary screen before you. The annotated script with your memory of the rushes are all the prompts you need. Make notes of this "pencil edit" so you can build it in the editing room with actual footage.

ASSEMBLY

If you shot standard coverage, all (or almost all) scenes will be covered in a single wide shot. Before diving into your pencil edit, cut together the best take of each wide shot in story order. Remove the slate and action/cut words. The onscreen story will be clunky, but it's there start to finish. This cut is called the "assembly."

On screening the assembly, ask yourself if your pencil edit notes are still on target. Are there new bumps in the story logic now that the scenes are assembled side-by-side? Any glaring omissions that may demand a re-shoot? At this point, make (more) notes.

ROUGH CUT

As soon as you cut the wide shot to insert coverage, you're building the rough cut. Dr. Structure will take a more active role from here on, evaluating the overall story and its details, including transitions between shots and scenes.

Wide shots are great for orienting the viewer in the room or space and for identifying key players in the scene. A movie, though, is not a stage play. In a movie, you move in close. Typically you'll move in for high stress moments, significant reaction shots, and facial expressions too subtle to be seen in a wide shot. You may also be forced to move in, or choose a shot from a new angle, to avoid poor performances or technical problems in the wide shot.

If your editing software allows you to save multiple versions of a sequence (like for music, several playlists using the same songs), dive in and experiment! If you can't save multiple choices, commit to the cut anyway. Trust your pencil edit notes for where and what to cut. Here, too, are a couple of tips to start you on the journey:

EDITING TIP: CUT ON MOVEMENT

As the camera should be invisible to the story during production, cutting between shots should be invisible during post. You want the audience to get into the story, not notice the editing. It's inherently jarring to blunt-cut from one image to a different image, so you're at a disadvantage. Whenever possible, cut on movement already happening in the frame. For example, cut during the character's act of standing,

Figure 24. Edit on movement—The image may not look well-framed at the end of Shot 1 and start of Shot 2, but it's the movement the viewer is watching.

Figure 25. Edit on movement—Final sequence.

act of sitting or during the turn of a head. (See figures 24 and 25.)

Cutting on movement accomplishes two things: (1) you distract the viewer from noticing the cut (because they are busy watching the character's movement), and (2) you can speed up or slow down the movement (standing, sitting, etc.) by slightly overlapping or trimming the action between the two shots. Who says you can't manipulate performances in the edit room? You are a master of time! Pro shoots use both multiple cameras and slow-motion to capture

Write! Shoot! Edit!   Deborah Patz

on-set explosions to fully maximize the on-screen time and drama of the effect. Watch for the overlap next time. Count the number of camera angles used that show the same action to really extend the duration of the effect or explosion on screen.

EDITING TIP: USE REACTION SHOTS

Make use of reaction shots (close-ups on the nonspeaking character in the shot). They have awesome power. You can take a reaction from one part of a scene and use it in another part of the scene. Once you lay the off-screen sound behind the shot in its new location, no one will know any different. Try adding a reaction shot where there was none mentioned in the script, or change a reaction from what was written and see what it does to the story.

You can also use reaction shots to extend the pacing of a scene, or to remove some spoken lines and tighten the pacing instead. In Chapter Six, I show how to use a reaction shot to fake a bow and arrow stunt (see figures 15 and 16). What other stunts could you create off-screen using reaction shots and sound effects?

The story is often told—and remembered—through the reaction shot.

Figure 26. The dissolve. Can you spot the slate in the shot dissolving in? Oops!

EDITING TIP: PLAN FOR FADES AND DISSOLVES

If you plan to start your movie with a fade in, and
then fade out at the end, make sure you have enough
moving picture for the duration of the fade. This type
of planning has to be done on set during the shoot.
The same forethought goes for dissolves (one image
fading out while another image fades in over it).
There must be sufficient overlap to cover the entire
fade out for the first shot and fade in for the second
one. You don't want to see the slate during the fade
or dissolve. (See Figure 26.)

EDITING TIP: REMEMBER SOUND

During picture edit, there are two things you can do
for sound. Take notes on sound issues as you notice
them. Will re-shooting a line of dialogue help? Also,
especially if music is integral to your movie, lay down
a track of rough or similar music to help properly
pace the story. You can replace the music with a final
piece later during sound edit.

When you think you're finished editing your picture,
there's one more stage to go.

FINE CUT

Allow Nitpicky Tweaker to step in at the fine cut. Trim frames as needed at start and end of shots to smooth out cuts and transitions. As the name suggests, think fine-tuning.

If you haven't already, draft a list of any missing parts that you can capture with a re-shoot.

At the end of the fine cut, consider the picture "locked." It's time to build the soundtrack.

Doin' it Again with Re-shoots

Are you missing a moment or a scene? Do you have a jarring jump cut because juxtaposed shots are from too similar an angle? Consider a re-shoot.

If possible, don't try to re-create the entire scene. That's too complex. Instead invent and capture a detail of the scene to use as a bridge shot to handle the problem.

In the case of a jump cut, the new material could be a cut-in to a prop on the table between the characters, or a cut-away to a close-up of a doorbell somewhere else in the house. Whatever you choose or design, the new shot must be logical to the story moment or it will jar the viewer more so than the jump cut.

Setting up a re-shoot day is nearly the same effort as setting up a shoot day, so review the Director's prep before embarking on such a path. Continuity pictures taken of the set, significant props and costumes will be a superb reference to re-create the necessary elements. Even if you could bring the editing computer onto the set for matching reference, it's time-consuming to search and find the moments you need. If you can get away without re-shoots, all the better, but sometimes, you just have to go there.

Fades, Dissolves and Other Post Effects

The editing software may tempt you with all kinds of post effects from fades and dissolves to wipes and watery image effects. In short, the fancier the visual effect, the more you draw the audience's attention away from the story to notice the effect. For scripted stories, it's traditional to fade in at the very start and fade out at the very end. Beyond that, you may not need any other effects. The odd dissolve between shots may be warranted if you need to indicate that time has elapsed in the story. Note that dissolves slow down the pace of the story to a more lyrical speed— not so great for action sequences.

Creative Credits

The start of the movie also displays the head credits. Tail credits are obviously the ones at the end. Since so many people are volunteering, it's worth giving everyone a screen credit.

For first films (especially short ones), the movie title is enough at the start of a movie so you can move on with the story. Use the tail credits to acknowledge all people and locations. Typically, the director's name comes first in the tail credits. If you are playing more than one role, reduce and hyphenate your jobs so your name doesn't show twelve separate times in the tail credits. For someone who is producer, writer, director, DOP, editor, lighting, etc., you can credit yourself as: Director/Writer/Editor and a second credit for Producer (which you might share with others who contributed money to your production's budget).

Use the editing software to lay text over image for screen credits. Making separate cards of names that fade in and out is technically easier than creating a credit roll like you see on feature films. Cards also give you the option of adjusting the duration of each one to ensure people can read their names. But . . .

This is a creative industry. Why not be creative with screen credits? Let Wild Inventor dream up some cool ideas. If, for example, there's a chess set as a feature prop in the story, why not use scrabble letters on a chess board? If there's a significant school theme to the story, why not use a chalk board and write the credits on the board? You can even cut between credits and shots from a gag reel, if you like, to keep the viewer watching all the way to the end. What are you going to invent?

Gag Reels

Speaking of gag reels . . . who doesn't love 'em? They seem so spontaneous, don't they? Ironically, they require more planning than you'd think.

The Continuity Supervisor on set can watch out for and flag funny moments on the set in the script notes. You may find, however, that you don't have enough to warrant creating an entire gag reel. Think of how short they are for Hollywood movies—and those movies shoot for weeks and months.

So, instead of a gag reel, how about a planned and staged backstage reel? Interview the performers in-character about life after fade out. Have each cast member mime to the feature song used in the movie. Stage mock auditions for the roles. Come up with something unique and thematic to the tone of your movie's story.

Sounds like a serious amount of planning to create a gag reel? Rest assured that at the premiere party, these gag or backstage reels are hysterical and so worth every second.

But we're not ready for the premiere yet. The sound post and finishing aren't done yet.

You are following the path of Editor! Go to
Chapter Five: Your Visual Storytelling Toolbox (page 46).

Chapter Ten

The Last Word of Postproduction: Sound and Finishing

It's tough to choose what to talk about last. Sound post is at the end of the post workflow, but planning for it started all the way back at the very beginning. Don't treat sound as an add-on at the end of the process.

It's possible that you're a bit tired of the film by now. You've invented and read drafts while writing. You've shot the same action repeatedly from numerous angles and in multiple takes. You've replayed those takes over and over again to find the right editing point. Well, rest assured there is magic in crafting the soundscape in postproduction, and the output to final format is coming soon. I promise.

Don't Be "Fixing it" in Post

We've talked a lot about providing flexibility of choice for post while you're shooting (overlapping action between shots, capturing room tone before wrapping the location, etc.). Those choices might make you think you can fix pretty much everything in the edit room. Not true.

Okay, okay, it is possible to re-record a line or two to replace unintelligible dialogue, but re-creating background sound, matching microphone position and vocal volume, and synching the new line to existing mouth movements means the new line can stick out like the audio version of a sore thumb.

You're also right that, if you have enough time and money, you could go back and re-shoot the entire movie, but that's not really postproduction anymore, is it?

During the shoot, you collected all those pieces (images and sounds) because in post you don't have the option to go back for another take. What you have is what you have. Treat post—especially sound post— as adding depth and complexity to the movie.

Adding Depth with Layers of Sound

Having tested the post workflow from capture to finish (during preproduction), you know how many tracks of sound you can lay down during sound post. I will presume five: two for dialogue, two for sound and atmosphere, and one for music. It sounds like a lot of tracks, but it's not.

If you put too much visual information in the picture frame, the image becomes confusing. Not so with sound. Sound is cool that way. The more complexity you layer in, the more realistic it sounds. Imagine a park scene where you don't hear any birds, wind, dogs, playing kids, crunching footsteps and so on. Close your eyes and listen to the room you're in right now. I bet there's a host of background sounds you choose to ignore. Humans have selective hearing. To simulate selective hearing, play with the sound levels (how loud each track is) to focus the audience's aural attention where you want it. That's why you want as many separate tracks as possible—to set different sound levels for each.

PLAYING WITH DIALOGUE AND EFFECTS TRACKS

Most of your cuts will butt the images and sound next to each other. It's the easiest way to work and by all means go ahead. If, however, there is dialogue that needs tweaking (in level or quality), separate that character's audio onto a different track. Isolated, you can modify it. (See Figure 27.)

Figure 27. Dialogue separated onto A and B tracks lets you target and fix problematic sound.

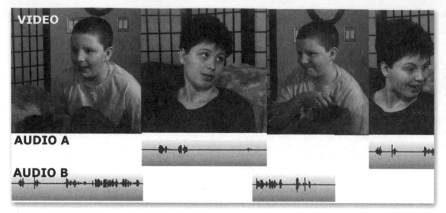

Figure 28. The amount of A and B dialogue track overlap lets you manipulate scene pacing.

Separate dialogue tracks let you quicken the delivery of dialogue by overlapping or near-overlapping lines intentionally. (See Figure 28.)

Think of sound separately from picture. You have the power to pick and choose the best picture and the best sound, and they don't have to come from the same take. Reaction shots (non-speaking characters) give you total freedom. Remove the sound from a reaction, and lay in the sound-only from another shot.

With this type of cut-and-paste, you may find a blank spot in your soundtrack. Blank spots are really obvious because of their lack of any type of sound whatsoever. For these cases, use a special effects track to lay down some room tone to cover up the space. (See Figure 29.)

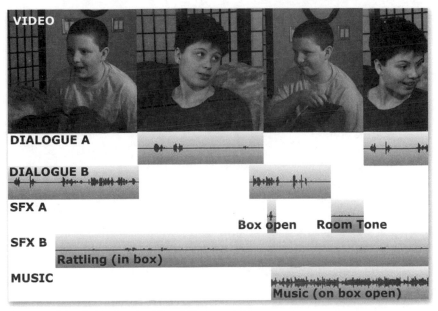

Figure 29. Fill audio blank spots with matching room tone.

ADDING SOUND EFFECTS

Watch the fine cut and make a wish list of the sound effects you could add.

Some sounds will be essential. These ones you can predict in the script, especially those that cause characters to react. When Middle C is stolen, for example, there has to be a sound effect to represent it.

Other sounds contribute to the soundscape and invite the audience into the room with the action. These sounds range from a light switch click and door closings to clothing rustles and footfalls as characters walk. How many of these you add will be determined by how much time you plan to spend in sound post. I give you fair warning. With every new sound effect you add, you'll be tempted to spend more time crafting and adding even more. Sound post is addictive.

Next, you have two choices to source those sound effects: download from a sound effects library or record it yourself.

There are many free online libraries to tap into for sounds you find problematic or downright impossible: large crowds cheering, creaky doors, stun guns . . . well, maybe not creaky doors. Upload them and checkerboard them into different effects tracks so you can tweak the volume or quality of each one individually.

You may, however, want to record your own effects (for fun or because the sound is too specific for a library). Sounds capture a little differently than the way you hear them in real life, but you know that already from hearing your own recorded voice played back to you. Am I right? The good news, then, is that it means you can invent sounds. Take stun guns. Nobody in Hollywood built one to record its sound. That sound had to be invented. Wave a large piece of sheet metal and I'll bet you "hear" thunder. Kiss your own arm and the sound could easily be that of two people kissing. Close your eyes, listen and create.

When it comes to the actual recording, use the original camera so that the sound is in the same technical format as the rest of the movie and super-easy to insert. For the picture element, use a full-frame slate at the start— or all the way through—to visually tell you in post what the recorded sound is.

A Special Note About Music

Music is not unlike sound effects but warrants special attention. Do you have background music, or is it part of the story and on-screen characters are performing it?

If you have performers miming to music, use music playback on set with a device separate from the camera. The sound you record on set will only be a "guide" track, so if it's of rough quality, that's okay as long as it's functional. Replace the guide track with the original (higher quality) sound file in post. Adjust the sound level so that the music doesn't overpower the rest of the soundtrack.

If you're cutting between a full-frame performance and a dialogue scene that puts the performance in the background, use two music tracks with the same music. For the full-frame performance shot, keep the volume high. For the dialogue scene, reduce the volume so the dialogue can be clearly heard. The

Figure 30. With the same music cut onto two tracks, the volume can be set to match the visuals.

visual cut from full-frame performance to performance in the background will perfectly match the change in audio level from full-frame loud to background soft. (See Figure 30.)

A final note about music: If you're writing and performing it, you own it. No problem. If you use someone else's recording, they own it and you need their permission, especially if you someday plan to share your movie publicly or over social media. More complex than that, the person who wrote and performed the music may not own all the rights to give you permission! For a first film like this, you may be lucky and not be sued for using someone else's music, but that's because you don't have much money. The people around you (like your parents) could be sued in your stead and you could be ordered to never distribute the movie. Not pleasant. It's a risk not worth taking. Either don't distribute your movie publicly, or enlist a budding musician among your friends to supply original music and permission (in writing, of course).

Finishing Formats for Today and Tomorrow

Can you believe it? You're ready to output the file to finished format! Unfortunately, with computers, yesterday's top-of-the-line is today's minimum standard and tomorrow's antique. Who knows what the future holds, but you'll want your file to be backwards-compatible enough to watch your movie years from now.

Output to the format you plan to watch today—maybe that's still DVD for you. Test a first copy to make sure the output worked successfully. Use this copy at the premiere screening with cast and crew. Next, make enough copies to gift to everyone you promised, plus a spare for yourself.

Plan, too, on archiving your material for the future. It may be hard to think that far in advance, but I promise you that years from now you'll want to watch this movie again. Beyond the finished digital output file, keep all the rushes (every scene, shot and take) if you can. Choose a digital format with no compression (like .avi) or the least compression possible. Compression reduces file size but reduces quality at the same time. In the future, you're going to need as much of that quality as possible. That may mean you need an external hard-drive to house all uncompressed digital files. Archiving is money well spent, but at least storage drives, like all computer elements, grow bigger and cheaper all the time . . .

. . . and this movie is only the beginning for you, isn't it? Ready to screen it with a crowd?

You are following the path of Editor! Go to
Chapter Eleven: Your Premiere and Future (page 135).

Write! Shoot! Edit! Deborah Patz

Chapter Eleven:

Your Premiere and Future (aka The Conclusion)

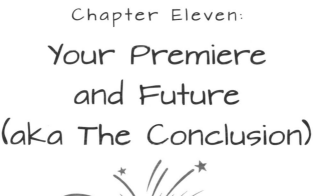

CONGRATULATIONS! YOU MADE A MOVIE. CELEBRATE!

Invite cast and crew to come to a private premiere followed by a party in true Hollywood style. Plan to screen the movie more than once because chances are there will be so many behind-the-scenes stories shared during the screening that key moments and great lines will be missed. If you made a gag or backstage reel, screen it between the two showings. Finally, take this opportunity to thank the team one more time for being part of the magic and present them with a copy of the movie.

Once the dust settles from the premiere, cast your mind back a bit. Was movie-making easier or harder than you thought? I'll bet you made a couple of surprising discoveries about your abilities along the way. Can't wait to do it all again? Whether your answer today is yes or no, plan a little break before starting again. During this "between time," reflect on the experience. Scribble notes in this book of things you'd do differently or better next time. Star or highlight new challenges that intrigue you. Even if you plan an equivalent sequel to your current story, sequels always try to outshine their predecessors.

Who knows where this movie will take you? Whatever path you chose last time, try a new one next time. Even if you chose multiple paths, read the book in a new order to shake your perspective a bit. Yes, you've called "It's a wrap!" on this movie, but as you know now, wrap on one thing is only the start of something new. Will your something new be writing, shooting and/or editing?

Enjoy your
cinematic journey!

Glossary

I've explained terms in context throughout the book when explanations are most relevant. In case you've forgotten some and want to use 'em like a pro, here's a refresher plus an index of where to find them. For other terms that boggle you, connect with me at my website and F.I.L.M. & I.N.K. Blog: www.debpatz.com or on Facebook: www.facebook.com/DebPatzBooks.

3-Act Structure (p. 31)—A term that describes the story structure typically used for scripts. Act One introduces the main characters and the story problem. Act Two (twice as long as Act One) develops the story using a roller coaster of events. Act Three brings all the elements together into the climax and to resolve the story problem. Each act ends with a (hopefully surprising) story twist.

Block (p. 100)—It's the first stage of the shoot day structure. Blocking is when you walk the performers through a scene, identify and mark their key stopping points, and place the camera for the first shot.

Coverage/Footage (p. 72)—Coverage is the collection of shots and takes you have to capture the scene's action. "Standard coverage" is a term to describe the typical scenario where you shoot a wide shot of the entire scene, then move the camera in to shoot the scene again using close-ups of each performer. Standard coverage gives the Editor plenty of choices in shots and angles when cutting the scene in the edit room.

Craft Service (p. 96, Figure 22)—Okay, I don't really explain this one in the book. Craft Service is snacks and drinks available on set to tide the cast and crew over until a meal break. It's essential to boost the morale on set and prevents growling stomachs from ruining the sound on a shot.

DOP (p. 2)—A short form for Director of Photography (the key crew member in the camera department).

DP (p. 2)—Another short form for Director of Photography (the key crew member of the camera department). It also happens to be my initials!

Implied Scene (p. 49)—It's a scene that's not in the script or finished film, but from watching the scenes that are there, it's obvious the action in the implied scene happened off-screen. Implied scenes help you quicken the pace of the screen story.

Juxtaposition (p. 52)—One of my all-time favorite words, so I just had to include it again. It's a fancy word for putting two things together side-by-side.

Doing so creates an effect that is more than the sum of the two parts. It's the magic of movies.

Post (p. 10)—A short form of "postproduction." It's the editing stage and starts on Day 2 of principal photography when you can start to cut the first scenes together and ends when the movie is delivered to its final destination: the premiere!

Prep (p. 8)—A short form of "preproduction." It's the time spent preparing for the shoot, gathering all the parts from script to cast and crew to props and locations and on and on.

Principal Photography (p. 9)—An impressive term for "the shoot." It starts the first day you start filming the script and ends the last day you capture the final shot. Pick-up shots and re-shoots can be captured during postproduction, but that's not principal photography anymore.

Production (p. 98)—This word is used to describe the creation of the entire film (I'm working on a film production = I'm making a movie), or it's used as another term for principal photography (I'm in production on my movie = I'm shooting my movie right now).

Rehearse (p. 102)—There are two times that you rehearse: (1) during prep when the Director runs through the entire script with the cast, and (2) as the third stage of the shoot-day structure. Rehearsing each shot is done after blocking and lighting so the cast can run through the scene without a script and the crew can have a technical rehearsal before the camera rolls.

Room Tone (p. 110)—A totally essential sound element, room tone describes the so-called "silence" or white noise of a room or space. Record room tone at every shooting location no matter how quiet you think it is. When there is complete absence of sound in the soundtrack during editing (caused by choice and duration of shots), the Editor looks to lay down room tone to make the space sound empty, not missing.

Rule of Thirds (p. 65)—An imaginary tic tac toe grid in the camera's frame. The four intersection points are used as a guide to frame the subject in the shot, instead of framing everyone dead center. Off-center framing of the subject is both pleasing and used especially for dialogue scenes (where one performer will be off-center to the left and the other performer off-center to the right to provide the illusion they are talking to each other).

Scene (p. 98)—A script is divided into scenes so each one can be scheduled and shot separately; therefore, a scene break happens when the story has a change of space (triggering the cast and crew to move to a new location), or a change of time (triggering a costume or set-dressing modification).

Script Day (p. 88)—Days in a script differ from shooting days during principal photography. A script day is one day (and usually one costume change) in the script's story. They are numbered sequentially starting on the first page of the script, so Script Day 1 could be Monday afternoon, and Script Day 2 could be the following Saturday morning, and Script Day 3 could be a flashback scene to five years ago.

Setup (p. 99)—A setup is the placement of the camera and lighting equipment in order to capture a shot. Usually there is one shot per setup, but if you use the camera's zoom, you could have two shots using one setup.

Shoot (p. 102)—See Principal Photography.

Shot (p. 99)—A shot is a camera angle on the scene (close-up, wide shot, etc.). Though it's possible to shoot a scene in one shot, more typically, several shots are used to capture the action from various angles.

Slate/Clapboard (p. 99)—The slate is the cool-looking board with black and white-striped clapper on top. On the board, you write identifying information to the Editor, like the scene, shot and take numbers. By clapping the board shut, you provide a visual and audio cue for the Editor to sync picture to sound. If you're not recording sound on a separate machine from the camera, you don't need the clapper part . . . unless you want to use it anyway and look cool.

Take (p. 99)—A take is one attempt to capture a shot. Even if Take One is fabulous, you may choose to do a Take Two "for safety" because Editors love choice.

Workflow (p. 114)—Also known as "post workflow," it encompasses the series of technical steps required from image capture on set, through the editing stages and to the output of the final format. It's best to test the entire workflow functions perfectly during preproduction, when you have time to fix any technical problems you discover.

Wrap (p. 110)—On a film production, you can wrap a lot of things (that are not gifts). Declaring "It's a wrap!" means it's all done and it's time to clean up. To wrap a shot is to say it's okay to move the camera to a new spot. To wrap the day is to tell everyone to tidy up and go home for the night. To wrap the shoot is to declare that all scenes have been shot and principal photography is over; it's time to clean up and say goodbyes and farewells (until the premiere). Now, as for this book, well, we're at the very, very end, so . . . it's a wrap!

About the Author

Deborah ("Deb") Patz has been a professional in the film industry since the mid-1980s, with a filmography that spans family and children's programming, science fiction extravaganzas and feature films of various budget sizes.

She started making movies when she was 9 years old, pioneered a filmmaking course at high school (because they didn't have one) and even taught the teacher how to process film (so he included it in the course). After a BFA in Film Production at York University and years of working on productions with such companies as Disney, Lucasfilm, Alliance/Atlantis, Nelvana, MCA/Universal, and the IMAX space team, Deb penned her first books: *Surviving Production* and *Film Production Management 101* (known as the Swiss Army Knife of production management), also published by MWP. Based on her books, Deb has designed and instructed numerous courses, seminars and workshops in Canada, the US and UK, and has worked with young teens to help them make elaborate, scripted home movies.

She holds an MFA in Creative Writing from the University of British Columbia with a speciality in Children's and YA, works in film finance, and teaches first filmmaking workshops for teens. When not involved in making movies, you can find her sailing the Pacific Northwest with her family and two adorable but stubborn Westies.

You can connect with Deb through her website and F.I.L.M. & I.N.K. blog: www.debpatz.com or on Facebook at: www.facebook.com/DebPatzBooks

FILM PRODUCTION MANAGEMENT 2ND EDITION
MANAGEMENT AND COORDINATION IN A DIGITAL AGE

DEBORAH S. PATZ

Known as "the Swiss Army knife of production management," *Film Production Management 101* is actually two books in one — the essential open-on-the-desk guide for both production managers and coordinators. Patz takes you on a journey from development and pre-visualization to postproduction and audit, covering everything with detailed insights, humorous production stories and the inside scoop on working in film and television production.

Film Production Management 101 and Patz' previous *Surviving Production* were quickly adopted as "the" essential road map to the business and logistics of on-the-job film & television production since 1997. Originally developed from practical tools Patz created for her film and television production career, this new edition has undergone a comprehensive update to address the shifting balance between digital and film technologies and to pave the way as we progress further into the digital age. The book includes everything from budgeting, to managing the production office, to script revisions, to cost reporting, to copyright, to publicity, and much, much more. With Patz' penchant for sharing knowledge and her knack for communicating concepts, *Film Production Management 101* continues to be the book you have to have open on your desk for every prep, shoot, and wrap day. The more than 50 useful forms and checklists which are included (and downloadable) will save you time, money, and headaches, working like a pro right from day one.

"At last the complex relationship between the creation of a film and the day-to-day production management and coordination of that film is spelled out in clear, readable, and accurate detail. Deborah has written a wonderful book which should be extremely helpful to novice low-budget independent filmmakers and seasoned professionals alike."

> — Sharon McGowan, Independent Producer and Assistant Professor
> University of British Columbia Film Program

"An invaluable and comprehensive guide. Deborah Patz has drawn on her own experience and has written a thoroughly researched and helpful book."

> — Norman Jewison, Producer/Director, *The Hurricane, Moonstruck, Fiddler on the Roof*

DEBORAH PATZ has been a filmmaker on award-winning productions since the mid-1980s, primarily as a production manager and coordinator, and then as production executive. She has worked with Lucasfilm, IMAX, MCA/Universal, Alliance/Atlantis, Nelvana, BBC, CBC, the Disney Channel, and the list goes on.

$39.95 · 500 PAGES · ORDER NUMBER 147RLS · ISBN: 9781932907773

FILMMAKING FOR TEENS
2ND EDITION
PULLING OFF YOUR SHORTS

TROY LANIER & CLAY NICHOLS

BEST SELLER

With over 20 hours of video being uploaded to YouTube every minute, how can a young filmmaker possibly stand out? By reading and applying the tools of *Filmmaking for Teens* young filmmakers can learn everything they need to know about how to make a great short film.

The updated edition of this classic manual for young filmmakers includes numerous additions reflecting the enormous changes impacting the world of digital video.

New and up-to-date information on:
- shooting in HD
- advances in digital audio recording equipment
- editing and compressing video for online delivery
- maximizing your exposure on video sharing sites like YouTube
- marketing and audience development strategies for online video
- how to make money from the online video revolution

"*Filmmaking for Teens is an excellent textbook geared to the young reader but with sage advice that most professionals follow. The book is comprehensive yet simple and easily comprehended. Film production is not a simple task, but reading this text makes it approachable for the high school student. It demystifies a complicated field.*"

> — Jane Jackson, Assistant Chair of the Communication Department,
> State University of New York

"*Filmmaking for Teens, 2nd Ed. makes for an easy read with loads of information in a concise way. This book will give you the edge you need to get a jump-start into the world of film. A perfect book for starting filmmakers.*"

> — Erin Corrado, www.onemoviefiveviews.com

TROY LANIER and CLAY NICHOLS have gone on to become pioneers in the online video industry. Producers of the acclaimed series *DadLabs*, the pair has produced over 500 episodes of web TV that have garnered millions of viewers. They will be using this platform to promote *Filmmaking for Teens*, 2nd edition to parents and kids alike though the creation of a series of web videos, shared on both the extensive DadLabs distribution network, and on a dedicated YouTube channel. The masters of online video practice exactly what they preach based on the principles of this book.

$26.95 · 240 PAGES · ORDER NUMBER 132RLS · ISBN 13: 9781932907643

THE MYTH OF MWP

In a dark time, a light bringer came along, leading the curious and the frustrated to clarity and empowerment. It took the well-guarded secrets out of the hands of the few and made them available to all. It spread a spirit of openness and creative freedom, and built a storehouse of knowledge dedicated to the betterment of the arts.

The essence of the Michael Wiese Productions (MWP) is empowering people who have the burning desire to express themselves creatively. We help them realize their dreams by putting the tools in their hands. We demystify the sometimes secretive worlds of screenwriting, directing, acting, producing, film financing, and other media crafts.

By doing so, we hope to bring forth a realization of 'conscious media' which we define as being positively charged, emphasizing hope and affirming positive values like trust, cooperation, self-empowerment, freedom, and love. Grounded in the deep roots of myth, it aims to be healing both for those who make the art and those who encounter it. It hopes to be transformative for people, opening doors to new possibilities and pulling back veils to reveal hidden worlds.

MWP has built a storehouse of knowledge unequaled in the world, for no other publisher has so many titles on the media arts. Please visit www.mwp.com where you will find many free resources and a 25% discount on our books. Sign up and become part of the wider creative community!

Onward and upward,

Michael Wiese
Publisher/Filmmaker